FUNDING
MINISTRY
with
FIVE LOAVES
and
TWO FISHES

ROSARIO PICARDO

FUNDING MINISTRY

with

FIVE LOAVES

and

TWO FISHES

FOREWORD BY MIKE SLAUGHTER

Abingdon Press
Nashville

ISBN: 978-1-5018-1892-9

16 17 18 19 20 21 22 23 24 25—10 9 8 7 6 5 4 3 2 1
MANUFACTURED IN THE UNITED STATES OF AMERICA

CONTENTS

FOREWORD

Even before Pastor Rosario (Roz) Picardo recently started shaving his head, he was almost bald. So why was he in his neighborhood barbershop in Trotwood, Ohio, every Monday like clockwork? Because Roz knew that the barbershop in his largely African American neighborhood was a popular hub of community connection and camaraderie—and Roz was determined to reach his neighbors for Jesus.

Roz used this same "leave no stone unturned" drive as a parachute-drop pastor in Lexington, Kentucky, when he started a church in a movie theater with no people and next to no money. That church plant soon became a multisite movement serving hundreds of people in at-risk urban areas. Now, as executive pastor of New Church Development at Ginghamsburg United Methodist Church, Roz is actively dreaming, designing, and deploying a network of leaders and churches that will reach the lost and set the oppressed free, both in our own Dayton, Ohio, backyard and in points well beyond.

In *Funding Ministry on Five Loaves and Two Fishes*, Roz moves readers beyond simple theory and theology, providing struggling pastors and church leaders with practical methods for doing powerful ministry and mission on a dime. Roz understands that casting a compelling vision, then using what's already in your hand, leveraging partnerships, and remaining relentlessly focused on the mission of Jesus are the essentials of making effective new wineskins in our post-Christian twenty-first century.

Funding Ministry with Five Loaves and Two Fishes is a great read and a dynamic tool that will empower and equip courageous, entrepreneurial leaders to create new, renewed faith communities that will reach the world for Jesus.

—Mike Slaughter

PREFACE

Clergy are trained to preach, teach, and lead a congregation in their spiritual lives. However, when it comes to the business aspects of church leadership—finances, debt reduction, fund-raising, and building maintenance—the lack of training that clergy receive is increasingly alarming. This added and, sometimes, unexpected dimension of pastorship can become cumbersome and stressful, even in financially healthy churches. Add to this lack of training the overall decline of the church and the death of a generation of faithful givers, and many pastors are saddled with crumbling churches and few resources to do anything about it.

I have found myself in this exact position: from starting a church in a movie theater with no people and little financial support, to revitalizing a dying congregation in a deteriorating physical structure, to serving as executive pastor for new church development with Ginghamsburg Church. Through trials and failures, I've explored innovative avenues for doing ministry and learned to think entrepreneurially. God has provided, and I've found new approaches for reaching and growing disciples of the lost even in the least promising financial circumstances.

In *Funding Ministry with Five Loaves and Two Fishes*, I share the lessons I've learned. The church is not dead; it's just time for a new wineskin. This book is for any pastor, church planter, or lay leader hungry to minister to the lost with the good news of Jesus Christ while struggling with a lack of financial resources.

I want to give a special shout-out to some folks who have helped me develop my thoughts in this project: my lovely wife, Callie Picardo, and colleagues Erin McKenzie, Justin Barringer, Christy Wade, LeTicia Preacely, Tracey Obenour, and Shannon Sampley. Thank you for all your help.

WHAT THEY DON'T TEACH PASTORS

I remember feeling confused and uneasy about what was going on. I kept flipping pages and somehow missing what everybody else was talking about. Everyone around the table seemed to have a clue except me. Then it dawned on me: I was the only one who couldn't read and understand the expense report, let alone the columns in the Excel spreadsheet. I felt embarrassed and grossly unprepared for the first pastoral role I had embarked upon. Seminary had prepared me to preach, order the church in polity, serve my community, and share in the sacraments. But nobody ever mentioned that I would need to know the first thing about finances, human resources, building maintenance, and capital campaigns. Pastors farther along in their career don't get special training on these things either; only experience teaches them. Many pastors delegate these roles, leaving decisions up to the finance committee, trustees, pastor-parish relations, or an HR committee, trusting their judgment and hoping nothing goes wrong. But what if something does go wrong? It wouldn't matter much to the bishop or district superintendent whether it was the fault of the pastor, the treasurer, the finance committee, or the trustees.

The pastor is the leader and is held accountable. I realized quickly in that first role that I was ultimately responsible for a lot more than I had bargained for.

After that initial finance meeting, I made a vow to myself not only to invite trusted people with calling, capacity, character, chemistry, and competency into servant-leadership positions, but also to educate myself about what was taking place in the church's physical life: its space, its systems, its structures, and its money. It was time to start my own training program by having discussions with colleagues in the business world, reading pertinent articles, watching economic trends, and paying close attention to what was coming into and going out of my local church.

People frequently say that the church is not a business—implying either that clergy need not concern themselves with knowledge of sound financial practices (let alone endeavor to put such practices into place in their churches), or that church finances are not subject to the same economic forces felt elsewhere in the economy. What is typically meant by this assertion is that the church is not in the business of making a financial profit. Rather, the church's business—its primary mission—is "to make disciples of Jesus Christ for the transformation of the world."[1] No pastor will argue this point. Yet, the "wineskin" of this mission is the local church, and the local church is sustained by the hard-earned money it receives from its faithful contributors and members. Any organization that solicits, receives, and handles money is, by definition, a business. To say that the church is not in business to make a profit, while true, does not offer an excuse for substandard financial practices. If anything, nonprofits like churches ought to adhere to higher standards of fiscal responsibility and transparency than their for-profit counterparts. The worst mistake a nonprofit can make is to think like a nonprofit. Pastors spend years of training to better understand the Bible, worship, discipleship, missions, and evangelism. The local church expects pastors to be gifted in these areas and to practice these gifts with excellence. But in order to guide the church as a whole in the future, congregations need to better anticipate the need for clergy to be trained as financial leaders of their churches as well.

The issue of financial illiteracy or apathy among clergy is exacerbated by today's economic realities. It's nothing new to hear the church is in decline in America, but the statistics are manifesting into tangible realities in many of our churches. Seasoned pastors who made it by with little focus on the physical aspects of their churches, or who simply deferred needed structure maintenance, are now feeling the pinch from the recent recession. Large churches with surpluses at the end of 2015 now have to make cuts and get creative with their programming. Revenue is decreasing with the passing of generations of faithful givers, and current generations carry a larger financial load than those who came before them. All the while, expenses continue to grow.

Taken together, the future can look pretty grim. However, turnaround is possible. Reaching a brighter and more sustainable future will require the clergy to gain financial fluency and acumen, to take calculated entrepreneurial risks, and to commit to their own financial freedom and giving before asking it of their congregations.

The average person carries debt today because debt has become the "American way." Pastors know that God's people should set the example of stewarding resources. The hitch is that, like other college graduates, pastors emerge from seminary and Bible college with enormous debt loads that they have no idea how to manage—some to the tune of over $100,000. Without insight about how to reach their own financial freedom, clergy are promptly thrown into churches to manage six- or seven-figure budgets. Often these pastors also inherit century-old buildings complete with deferred maintenance and skyrocketing utility bills. (The real estate euphemism "Needs love!" comes to mind.) These traditional buildings that once reached the masses have become dead weight to clergy; in many cases, they are no longer hospitable to the very communities they were built to serve. Budgets and buildings have become some of the biggest barriers between clergy and successful ministry in a post-Christian culture.

Because budgets and buildings can demand so much time, attention, and resources, many pastors are torn between these pressing administrative needs and the numerous, more traditionally "pastoral" needs they see in their surrounding community. Too often, the resources left over to meet the needs of the community are limited.

Jesus's disciples must have felt similar as they were faced with a hungry crowd of five thousand men and perhaps an additional five to ten thousand women and children! Then, to hear Jesus ask, "Where do you suppose we get the food to feed our new friends?" would have freaked out any of his disciples. However, Andrew spotted what little was in front of him, a boy's lunch of five small barley loaves and two small fish. Andrew mentioned these items—perhaps sheepishly or facetiously—with no expectation that the impossibly small parcel of food would be multiplied to feed the crowd, but instead simply as an answer to Jesus's question. Those loaves and fish were the only resources at hand. The most obvious miracle was the multiplication of the food. But Andrew's willingness to speak up and potentially look foolish in front of Jesus was another miracle. Andrew thought outside the box and utilized what was plainly in front of him. To learn how to multiply the resources God has laid in front of you for the mission of making

4

disciples for Jesus Christ, as you read this book, I would urge you to think differently and courageously about the business side of the local church.

If Jesus were to look into your eyes and ask you, "How do we meet the needs of our friends in this community?" what would you tell him? The need may seem staggering, but the answers could be right in front of you.

As a team of young clergy starting out with little financial background, by God's grace, we were able to plant a parachute-drop church in a movie theater for a weekly rental rate of $130. There was a void of churches that allowed people to be authentic and real. Being in the Bible Belt, many churches were associated with being "religious"; we wanted to start one that broke that stereotype so people could have a real encounter with Jesus and be introduced into a relationship with him. As that church grew, the denomination gave us a dying church with deferred maintenance, and, as the Lord guided us, it became an epicenter in a gentrifying community. We cast a God-shaped vision that compelled both full-time and bi-vocational staffers to raise support.

Currently, God has me planting another congregation in an urban shopping center in partnership with a local megachurch and community organizations. The shopping strip is owned by the local district of the United Methodist Church. Several churches have started and failed in this location. After the most recent failure the district superintendent offered the location to Ginghamsburg United Methodist Church, and as their executive pastor of new church development, I was tasked with bringing a church back to life in this space. In the brief time this congregation has existed, it has been able to help the area restore a sense of community and goodwill through meeting needs that present themselves, taking advantage of partnerships, and ministering on a budget.

5

This book will highlight the inspiring ways pastors are doing ministry on five loaves and two fish. As we continue our journey together, we will use the story of Jesus feeding the many as a backdrop:

> After this Jesus went across the Galilee Sea (that is, the Tiberias Sea). A large crowd followed him, because they had seen the miraculous signs he had done among the sick. Jesus went up a mountain and sat there with his disciples. It was nearly time for Passover, the Jewish festival.
>
> Jesus looked up and saw the large crowd coming toward him. He asked Philip, "Where will we buy food to feed these people?" Jesus said this to test him, for he already knew what he was going to do.
>
> Philip replied, "More than a half year's salary worth of food wouldn't be enough for each person to have even a little bit."
>
> One of his disciples, Andrew, Simon Peter's brother, said, "A youth here has five barley loaves and two fish. But what good is that for a crowd like this?"
>
> Jesus said, "Have the people sit down." There was plenty of grass there. They sat down, about five thousand of them. Then Jesus took the bread. When he had given thanks, he distributed it to those who were sitting there. He did the same with the fish, each getting as much as they wanted. When they had plenty to eat, he said to his disciples, "Gather up the leftover pieces, so that nothing will be wasted." So they gathered them and filled twelve baskets with the pieces of the five barley loaves that had been left over by those who had eaten.
>
> When the people saw that he had done a miraculous sign, they said, "This is truly the prophet who is coming into the world." Jesus understood that they were about to come and force him to be their king, so he took refuge again, alone on a mountain. (John 6:1-15)

Chapter 1

WHY SO HUNGRY?

Debt is the slavery of the free.

—Publilius Syrus (Roman author, 1st century BCE)

When the crowds learned this, they followed him on foot from the cities. When Jesus arrived and saw a large crowd, he had compassion for them and healed those who were sick. That evening his disciples came and said to him, "This is an isolated place and it's getting late. Send the crowds away so they can go into the villages and buy food for themselves." (Matt 14:13-15)

Increasing Debt, Decreasing Funding

Before diving into the assets, solutions, and innovations pastors and congregations may already have at hand without realizing it, it would be beneficial to first discuss the factors of financial trouble currently plaguing so many pastors and congregations. Many readers have probably experienced firsthand one or several of these factors, each one compounding the others. But fear not! After a look at the issues, the focus will shift to the loaves and fish waiting for God's multiplying power in our hands.

The first issue facing many pastors is that they are graduating from seminary with dramatically high student loan debt. This issue is itself multifaceted. First, due to their own increasing expenditures and decreasing financial support, seminaries are less able to assist in funding their students' tuitions. Students must therefore rely on loan-based financial aid that they will pay back with interest. Second, pastors are required to complete lengthy degree programs in order to be successful candidates in their denominations. Denominational bodies frequently require credentialing beyond the master of divinity. The psychological exams, clinical pastoral education, and internships required for pastor candidacy force more debt on pastors. The results are summarized in an article titled "The Gathering Storm," written in 2005 by the Auburn Center for the Study of Theological Education.[1] This report found that in 2001 only 37 percent of master of divinity students graduated from their seminary education without having to borrow student loans, compared to 1991 when more than half were able to graduate without borrowing money. Of the seminary students who graduated in 2011 with a master of divinity degree, more than 25 percent amassed forty thousand dollars or more in educational debt, and 5 percent accumulated eighty thousand dollars or more in debt. Some have even suggested cutting the required seminary degree in half to reduce debt for new pastors.[2]

This leads us to our next set of obstacles. Job openings for a full-time pastor are difficult to find, and the jobs that are available pay a salary that makes it challenging or impossible for a new seminary graduate to make his or her monthly loan repayments. Consider my friend and former colleague Justin Barringer. In July 2014, *The Atlantic* ran an article detailing Justin's inability to find a full-time pastor position. Despite an impressive résumé with a seminary degree, pastoral and missionary experience, and published works, Justin searched for two years and applied to nearly a hundred jobs without receiving a full-time offer.[3] To add to his complications, this young pastor had an enormous amount of student loan debt. He not only lacked enough for a meal, but he owed his creditors more than some bread and a few small fish. Unfortunately, Barringer's story is not uncommon these days.

Those who are fortunate enough to secure a full-time church pastor position will join a profession with an average annual wage of $43,800,[4] despite a required education level similar to that of doctors, lawyers, and other professionals. While pastors don't need or generally even desire to become wealthy as they work for the church, churches must recognize that when a pastor comes out of seminary with significant debt, his or her options for job placement are limited. Not only are pastors looking for the right places to serve, but they are also looking for positions that pay enough to enable them to manage their student debt. Yet congregations often cannot afford to pay pastors at levels necessary to pay off the increasing debt required to fund a theological education. This often puts pastors in the problematic position of finding additional sources of income, whether that means working two jobs to cover personal bills, feeding their families with federal assistance programs, or both.

A third, crucial dimension to the state of financial distress in which many of the clergy and their churches find themselves is the lack of financial training given to or expected of pastors, despite the real need that exists for such training. There is both a personal and a congregational element to this for pastors. How well-equipped can a new seminary graduate be to handle a church's finances—sometimes a budget of six or seven figures, often when the church is already financially burdened itself—without the first notion about how to manage his or her own combined student loans and personal debt? And yet, this is exactly the position many new pastors find themselves in today. Pastors are expected to lead their congregations in living faithful Christian lives, and financial stewardship is not exempt from this charge. A standard master of divinity program ranges from seventy-five to one hundred or more credit hours and includes courses on biblical languages, philosophy, exegesis and hermeneutics, ethics, church history, pastoral care and counseling, spiritual formation, sacramental theology, systematics, and communication—to name a few! However, seminaries and denominations are not adequately preparing pastors in the areas of financial stewardship. Pastors often lack a robust, theological account of money and the practical preparation necessary to steward either their own finances or the finances of their churches.

In light of such a cycle, and in combination with the decline in church membership and offerings, one can begin to sense the same overwhelming bewilderment or even dread the disciples might have felt when Jesus asked, "Where will we buy food to feed these people?" (John 6:5). Yet, like Jesus's earliest disciples, pastors and churches must trust that God brings abundance from scarcity. "Jesus said this to test him, for he already knew what he was going to do" (v. 6).

Jesus already knew that the many would be fed—and how it would happen. But he asked his disciples to faithfully take stock of what was at hand. In this way, God also asks us to participate by recognizing the gifts each person has to offer and trusting that God can multiply those gifts exponentially.

Pastors as Financial Leaders

When I started out as a young pastor, I had no idea how to read a spreadsheet, let alone manage an entire church budget. By

God's grace, I am now married to a lady who is incredibly gifted in financial management, and is in fact the director of development operations at a respected seminary. But back in those early days, I simply did not have a clue. I knew I wanted to serve God by serving and leading others, but I had no idea that doing so would require me to be more faithful with my own finances in order to help my congregation be faithful with the little money we had. If there was an area where my seminary education and life experience up to that point had failed me, it was in the realm of money. However, over time I learned that the use of money can glorify God and advance God's kingdom—or it can cause us to stumble. Personal finances, church finances, and stewardship must be a priority to the pastor. As ministers, our attitudes toward money will be reflected in our churches' attitudes toward finances. We should strive to be above reproach with regard to our personal finances in addition to being better financial navigators for our churches.

When I met my wife, Callie, I realized I had a lot I could learn from her about finances. There are hundreds of reasons I fell in love with this woman, but her financial knowledge has been a blessing on top of everything else. After we were engaged, she made it a prerequisite to go through the Crown Financial Ministries small group study with her, if I wanted to marry her. As I studied in depth what God's word says about finances, I not only grew in my faith and personal finances but also developed convictions that have shaped how I lead the church. Callie also let me marry her, and the Bible study helped us start out the financial side of our marriage on the same page.

So how do pastors become better stewards of their personal finances? Despite challenges, there are simple, practical ways to accomplish this. Jeanine Skowronski, a senior credit card analyst and reporter at Bankrate.com, recommends the following: "Go back to basics. Write your budget out. Find what things that you can cut so you have five, 10, 20 extra dollars each week that you can drop into a savings account that will add up over time."[5] Do whatever you have to do to reduce your debt load, even if that means you need to take a second job for a season. Tax refunds are a valuable, short-term savings plan for paying off debts or for building savings accounts. If you need help learning how to budget, check out books from the local library, follow Dave Ramsey, or consult Crown Financial Ministries or a financial planner.

Pastors may also be able to improve their personal finances through the Public Service Debt Forgiveness and income-based repayment programs. Public Service Loan Forgiveness (PSLF) is a program for federal student loan borrowers who work in certain job fields. If a church is registered as a 501(c)(3), its pastors are qualified to take advantage of this program. PSLF forgives remaining debt after ten years of eligible employment and qualifying loan payments. During those ten years, an income-based repayment (IBR) plan can help keep loan payments affordable with payment caps based on income and family size. For example, if a borrower earns below 150 percent of the poverty level for his or her family size, the required loan payment will be zero dollars. If he or she earns more, the loan payment will be capped at 15 percent of earnings above that amount.[6]

Along with taking care of personal finances, pastors are tasked with conducting the church's business, often facing pressure to do more with less. Again, because seminary does not prepare ministers in this area, we need to find other avenues for gaining the necessary knowledge. To that end, some have proposed incorporating more bi-vocational training into seminary education.[7] Longtime Duke theologian Stanley Hauerwas has said that one way the church can be more faithful with its finances is for all church members to disclose their salaries. Pastors can lead the way by talking about their own families' finances, disclosing not only how much money they bring in but also how they spend it.[8] At a recent pastors' conference, Shane Claiborne suggested that church leaders consider switching salaries with church custodians for a year as a way to express God's jubilee.[9]

Whether the solution is as creative (and challenging) as those suggested by Hauerwas and Claiborne, or whether it is more traditional, this extra financial pressure may provide pastors with an opportunity to reform the way churches view money and mission. In part, pastors can succeed in spite of their own debt and the financial pressures of their churches by encouraging others to avoid debt and by setting an example as they continue to give faithfully to the work of the church.

My fellow pastors and I do ministry because we are called to it; we do not do it for the money. But we do need to pay our bills. It is important for churches to realize that, as one pastor said, "He [or she] doesn't do it because you give him [or her] money; you give him [or her] money because he [or she] does it."[10] In other words, congregants should give faithfully and generously because they believe in the work their pastors and churches are doing, not because their pastors are employees. This shift in attitude and understanding might help pastors and their congregations be more faithful in how they go about giving and making money, which in turn could radically change the way they do ministry together as members of the body of Christ.

One of the most crucial things a pastor must do in order to successfully lead in the area of church finances is to become educated about business basics. While a church doesn't share the same goals as most traditional, for-profit businesses, leading a church does require some business management techniques. The most beneficial business management aptitudes a pastor can gain fall into two categories: financial skills and people skills. Chuck Zech, director of the Center for Church Management and Business Ethics at Villanova University, says, "[Pastors] don't need to be accountants, but they should know how to read a financial statement. They also need to develop their skills related to conflict resolution, collaboration, and motivation."[11] Some practical ways to gain these financial skills include reading business books, seeking a businessperson as a mentor, or taking a finance course. In addition, pastors should seek training in the areas of new media, marketing, and social media, which are critical to today's business culture.

Another essential way for pastors to lead their churches financially is to continue their own faithful giving, setting an example for their congregations. Perhaps one of the most disheartening factors of the church finance equation today is that so few church members are actually giving to their churches. One study shows that as few as 12 percent of people who claim to be committed Christians are tithing, let alone giving above and beyond a tithe.[12] If the church is to continue affording facilities, pastors, and ministries, then church members must meet their responsibility to give money to the efforts of the church. As Matthew 25:23 reminds us, when a group or individual is faithful with a little—even with their debt—God will entrust them with more. Pastors who creatively and diligently pour themselves and their resources into the work of the Lord can trust in God's faithfulness to use that effort and multiply it for the kingdom. When pastors fail to give, they make a declaration against God's faithfulness and set a negative precedent for their congregations. As one pastor asks, "How can we expect our parishioners to give when we aren't willing to give?"[13] Pastors would never tell their congregants to pray, read the Bible, or serve others, but then say, "However, I am not going to pray, read the Bible, or serve others, because I just don't have the time or energy." Likewise, pastors should not encourage people to give their financial resources while refusing to do so themselves, no matter how bad their personal financial situation might be. No sermon, Bible class, blog post, or conversation can counteract the negative example of a pastor who fails to give. On the other hand, a pastor giving faithfully declares that he or she trusts Jesus and his teachings on God's faithfulness and his followers' finances. Pastors bringing their loaves and fish, however few they may have, will be the biggest inspiration for the rest of the church to follow and offer up their resources as well.

Churches as Financial Stewards

In response to the *Atlantic* piece about Justin Barringer, *Sojourners* published an article arguing, "The church is in trouble because somewhere along the line our society 'outgrew' the traditional model for church and a new model has not yet been developed."[14] The current model has relied primarily on the generosity of churchgoers as they drop their money in the plate or give during special fund-raising campaigns (almost always for building projects). It seems clear that this model is unsustainable because church giving is declining among those still attending, and church attendance is also declining. Churches have smaller budgets, but there is at least as much work to be done as before. While the generous giving of pastors and their congregants is the place to start, innovative financial strategies that trust in God's faithfulness are also becoming a necessity for many churches.

Some new church plants have decided to forego the expense of having their own building, while other congregations are finding new ways to use their existing property to both minister to the community and generate income. Embrace, the church plant in Lexington, Kentucky, drew from both strategies. We first began meeting in my home, then eventually moved to a movie theater for our Sunday worship gatherings, which meant we had virtually no overhead for facilities. While the theater was only available to us at select times, it was a convenient and spacious meeting place located in the center of town. When Embrace merged with another congregation meeting in a decades-old building, we gained a facility that we could use anytime, but we suddenly became responsible for enormous maintenance costs. First we asked ourselves how the spaces would be best used for ministry, but soon we were asking how we would pay to keep them up and running.

Many churches spend around a quarter of their budget on their buildings and land, yet they fail to utilize their property to its full potential. While many churches do lend out their space to local nonprofit organizations, there are countless other opportunities to use church space as a ministry center for the community as well as a revenue generator.[15] Having property means being able to use it in creative ways: housing a social enterprise, renting it out for events, hosting community meetings, sharing it with ministry partners, and perhaps even selling some of it to finance other ministry opportunities.

After Embrace found a home in the old church building, we decided to find creative ways to utilize it to bless the community and bring in money. The congregation was already leasing space to one after-school program, so we decided to invite other community groups to use the building as well. We rented out the sanctuary for concerts, the kitchen for cooking classes, and an upstairs classroom for another after-school program. Eventually, we sold some of our property for an innovative mixed-income apartment complex. The church was able to offset general operating expense by 20 percent because of these alternative revenue streams.

Other churches are also renting or selling their facilities in order to do more effective ministry and connect with their communities. For example, a Lutheran church in Grand Rapids, Michigan, sold its beautiful neo-Gothic building, and gave up certain luxuries like their pipe organ, in exchange for simplicity and the chance to better reach the city for Jesus. They decided to make people, rather than a building, their priority.[16] Of course, for some congregations the best way to make people a priority is to use their current buildings in a way that blesses people and makes good ministry sustainable. However an individual congregation decides to use its building or land, it must go with God and with the heart to serve others in the name of Jesus. In this way, the church will be like the little boy with his loaves and fish, ready to share them or give them up for the sake of a community.

Another obstacle that churches face with their limited budgets and ever-increasing needs is recruiting and maintaining called and competent staff. Staffing is the largest expense of most churches. Embrace sought to build a team of fund-raising and bi-vocational pastors to lead the ministry. Of the five pastors on the team, two were raising support for their salaries, and two were bi-vocational. The other pastor worked doing consulting for other church planters, as well as for the Kentucky Conference of The United Methodist Church, so that Embrace would bear less financial burden. The five bi-vocational pastors of Embrace Church's communities totaled $60,000, which resulted in quite a bit of savings considering the average compensation package for one ordained elder in the Kentucky Annual Conference in 2013 was $71,031 and the average ordained elder's package was $101,780.[17]

Another category churches spend within is programs and missions. This typically makes up about 15 percent of their budget.[18] Does this seem like a small percentage of the budget to be spending on the primary work of the church: evangelizing, discipling, and caring for the world around us? As a point of comparison, charity organizations and nonprofits are typically rated based on the percentage of their revenues put directly toward their goals. It is frequently considered a standard for these agencies to spend a bare minimum of one-third their revenues on their primary projects. While the comparison isn't apples to apples, it is nonetheless useful for churches to consider their income and spending similarly, committing to at least a specific percentage of revenue directly applied to outreach. This is one reason it is imperative for churches to find less expensive, but equally impactful, ways to do ministry. It is also another reason that churches need to reduce costs and increase revenues in other areas. If the church does not find ways to bolster its evangelism, discipleship, and mercy and justice ministries, it will experience an even swifter decline in membership, participation, and effectiveness than is currently forecast. Current trends of declining membership can be reversed, at least at the local level, if churches invest more in programs and missions. The old saying goes, "You have to spend money to make money," and it is similarly true that you have to pour effort and finances into your community, doing so with business savvy and creativity, all the while trusting in God for increase.

Buildings and pastors will continue to be significant financial responsibilities of the church. Congregations will need to find creative ways to use their property for financial gain and more effective ministry. They will also need to be more supportive of their pastors financially, emotionally, and practically, as pastors explore ways to support themselves and their ministries. God holds the future of the church in God's hands, and God calls each congregation and denomination to faithfully join in that future through new and innovative ministries that utilize every resource more effectively.

What the Future Might Hold

Psalm 50:10 tells us that God does not need our help. To offer a modern paraphrase, "God has a million dollars in a million banks." Jesus did not need a young boy's lunch, nor did he need his disciples' input. Nevertheless, he asked for both. Likewise, Jesus does not need our wisdom or our gifts, but he is calling pastors and laity alike to join in his mission on earth.

If the church is going to continue doing faithful ministry as its attendance and budgets decline, its people are going to be required to offer their gifts in ways they have not been required to do previously. Church members will need to give their expertise—from accounting to management, technology to networking, and beyond—in whatever capacity may benefit the church. Frankly speaking, church members will need to invest a lot more time in their congregations and fulfill their role in the priesthood of all believers.

With pastors often trained in a narrow field, receiving little guidance related to finance, organizational communication, technology, property maintenance, or management, other church members are needed to step into roles in these areas, or at least to help train their pastors to appropriately handle each of these important tasks. An accountant can help the pastoral staff with church finances. A contractor can help with building maintenance. An IT professional can help with technology like the church website. Contracting with outside experts in these areas can be prohibitively costly, so asking church members to serve in their areas of giftedness can save a congregation thousands of dollars. Even if a church can afford to staff according to its ministerial needs, the question becomes whether a church ought to staff this way. According to Lindsey Foster Stringer, financial coach and author, "Churches should have a pastor, staff member, or lay leader who is of personal integrity and financial good sense, available to teach, train, and coach members on the basics of managing money . . . someone with the financial skills and heart of a teacher."[19] Likewise, churches should have someone who trains others in areas such as building maintenance, technology, sound equipment, event planning, and so forth. These are all practical avenues for discipleship that will save the church money and invite more members to participate in the work of the Lord.

In Acts 6 the Bible shows us how diversification in leadership and delegation of responsibilities should work. The apostles were busy preaching the good news when they heard that Gentile widows were being overlooked as the church distributed bread. Rather than stop their preaching—the specific work to which they were called—in order to get food to these widows, the apostles appointed seven other men, "well-respected and endowed by the Spirit with exceptional wisdom" (Acts 6:3). In our times this could easily be translated into the various responsibilities of the church mentioned above. Every church needs people who are willing and wise, filled with the Spirit, to do glamorous and unglamorous tasks, to faithfully lead in a variety of areas as a way to make sure all needs are met at minimal cost to the church. This will free pastors to continue proclaiming the word and leading the congregation in prayerfulness, which will in turn serve to further the kingdom as word and deed are both blessings to the community.

When I entered ministry I could not have foreseen all of the areas where I would need to learn and grow. Probably like a lot of young pastors, I thought that my seminary training would be enough to help me lead a church. In reality, I'm not sure I even had five loaves and two fish at the start of my pastoral ministry, but God has proven faithful to use the little I brought to the table, and to bring others around me with gifts of their own to offer. In the years that I have been a pastor, I have gained skills in budgeting, management, marketing, maintenance, and technology. God is increasing my own offerings of knowledge and skill while continuing to convict me to return those gifts to God so that God can use them to bless the multitudes.

If the church is going to thrive, things must change. Pastors need more diversified training. Churches need more diversified leadership. Pastors need to be more generous in their giving. Church members need to be more generous as well. Pastors need to be more creative in their vision. Church members need to be more open to creative solutions to ongoing problems. Pastors need to delegate. Church members need to step into their areas of gifting and do their part.

There is no one simple solution. Seminaries, denominations, congregations, and pastors will have to work together to find new and creative ways to save, serve, and spend alongside one another. In the following chapters I hope to provide more concrete ways that the church can continue doing great ministry in the coming decades, even as they increasingly have to do so on a tight budget. With God, a budget is no obstacle, only an opportunity for the church to show their faith while God, once again, shows God's faithfulness. If you ever think you or your church lacks the resources to serve others and share the gospel, just remember that Jesus fed thousands with a small boy's lunch.

Rather than just sitting back and hoping things will happen, let's try to be like Andrew, seeking out whatever resources may be available, considering how to best utilize the gifts of our fellow servants, and growing in our understanding of how God is working in every aspect of the church, including finances.

Chapter 2

MISSION DRIVES MINISTRY

Donors don't give to institutions. They invest in ideas and people in whom they believe.

—*G. T. Smith*

> Jesus looked up and saw the large crowd coming toward him. He asked Philip, "Where will we buy food to feed these people?" Jesus said this to test him, for he already knew what he was going to do.
> Philip replied, "More than a half year's salary worth of food wouldn't be enough for each person to have even a little bit." (John 6:5-7)

The first step to a vibrant church is to act on a compelling, God-inspired vision and mission, then to articulate this vision effectively to those inside and outside of the congregation. A clear vision and mission focuses the ministry's work on what is most important, filtering out work that may be good but is not in line with the ministry's spiritual DNA. Buy-in for the vision and mission of a congregation is crucial to organizational growth and health.

Scripture is clear about the importance of vision. Proverbs 29:18, Hosea 4:6, and Habakkuk 2:2 all point to the principle that when people have vision (through divine revelation, knowledge, and understanding), they are inspired to follow what is communicated and put back in order that which is out of order. Within the realm of ministry, there is much in the world that is out of order; a clear vision compels people to engage in the work at hand to make the community a better place. Without vision, the church becomes ineffective, stops reaching out to the community around it, and fails to follow the Lord. When people believe in the vision, they commit to the mission and become passionate about the work of the ministry. This is key in being effective as a congregation, since each congregation must rely heavily on volunteers—especially those who are passionate and wholeheartedly committed.

This chapter will demonstrate how two churches with very different organizational circumstances and different visions and missions are able to fulfill the work God has called them to by proactively pursuing financial stewardship practices that match their theologies. These practices naturally take on different forms in a small start-up church in Lexington, Kentucky, and a large, well-established church just north of Dayton, Ohio. Yet, in both faith communities, the commitment to pairing vision with financial innovation and responsibility in the service of God's work has led to the multiplication of loaves and fish.

Embrace Church

At Embrace Church (a church that started as a plant), the vision, buy-in, and passion are evident in its success as a young ministry. Embrace initially consisted of a number of trained ministers who chose to raise their own support in order to be part of the staff, as well as a significant group of laity whom some might refer to as "super-servants." The story at Embrace Church centers on servant-leadership. The lead pastor at Embrace was bi-vocational. As an ordained elder in the United Methodist Church, he voluntarily chose to draw below the minimum elder salary for his conference. Additionally, he held another position with his conference as a church plant coach, and he also owned a business as a coach for pastors. (So actually, he was really "tri-vocational.") For a period of about two years, five out of six pastors at Embrace Church earned income from other occupations so that the church would have more finances to devote to ministry. With six total pastors, we could ensure that the church's outreach efforts had designated pastor-leaders and therefore adequate care.

In *Ministry Makeover: Recovering a Theology for Bi-vocational Service in the Church*, I discuss how ministers can devote themselves to the workforce while leading vital congregations. It is important to note common patterns between each bi-vocational minister's story as a guideline: a sense of calling by God to do ministry in this way, a sense of community for accountability and belonging, a sense of being blessed by their role in spite of financial challenges for some and the demand on their time, and a passion for ministry and people.

In addition to a solid bi-vocational staff at Embrace, the lay leadership is another crucial component in the story. Lay leadership is the main driving force behind the finance team, the trustees, the personnel team, the administrative council, the children's ministry, the nursery, and a number of other ministries and events.

Embrace is located near Asbury Theological Seminary and a few other universities, so the congregation regularly contains students who are actively pursuing or contemplating going into vocational ministry. The church uses this to its advantage, as these young people are eager to find ministry opportunities. A few seminary students decided to take staff positions, with the knowledge that they would not receive a paycheck and would have to raise all financial support. Embrace was open to interns and was fortunate to consistently receive solid and passionate people who helped strengthen the ministry. Interns provided the opportunity to expand the staff without stretching the budget.

As a result, interns helped to lead in areas such as Christian education, audiovisual worship, outreach, youth ministry, children's ministry, and in the worship band. In return, the interns make lifelong connections, gain mentors who are ahead of them by anywhere from a few years to several life steps, learn more about their own calling and strengths, and receive experiential learning opportunities that complement their formal education.

In your church, there may also be young people (college and seminary students) who are contemplating a call into vocational ministry. Could your church serve as a training ground for them to test this call? College and seminary students would be eager to help do ministry at the church, especially if you can get them to buy into the vision of the church. There may even be some who would be willing to raise financial support in order to serve as staff members at the church. They could set up blogs to write about their ministries and ask donors to contribute to the work they are doing at the church.

Ginghamsburg Church

Ginghamsburg Church in Tipp City, Ohio, is also a model for doing big ministry in a time of financial struggle. This church achieves its ministries by casting big, compelling visions, involving its members in reshaping the vision as God leads each person or individual campus, and teaching comprehensively on money and stewardship while being transparent about the state of its finances as a whole. The people of Ginghamsburg have exemplified generosity, financial freedom, and a desire to engage with the long-term vision.

For the last ten years, Ginghamsburg Church has challenged families to remember the reason for celebrating Christmas through the Christmas Miracle Offering. It is easy to celebrate an American Christmas, one that has outgrown the idyllic Norman Rockwell scene. Americans are crazy for sales on Thanksgiving Day and steal hours from their employers on Cyber Monday in order to spend extraordinary amounts of money on the latest gadgets for even the youngest members of their family.

Each year, Ginghamsburg challenges families to give an amount, beyond their regular tithes and offerings, toward the Christmas Miracle Offering equal to what they spend on their own family's Christmas. This could mean that congregants give extravagantly or spend very little on their own families in order to give more: either way, it refocuses the family's attention on what is truly important.

The Christmas Miracle Offering is used to fund projects that meet real-life needs, primarily the Sudan Project. In Sudan, civil war has raged for years between Muslims and Christians in what the United Nations has labeled "the worst humanitarian crisis in the world."[1] To bring the Sudan Project to the forefront of the congregation's consciousness, Ginghamsburg has preached untraditional Advent sermon series and decorated for Christmas with bare tree branches, thatch huts, and batik fabrics. The church has displayed monitors on stage that count the number of children who die of malaria during a single worship celebration and have sent teams to Sudan to capture reality on the ground and bring back stories that authorities would not allow to be filmed.

Members have responded to the message. Life groups have gathered unused items from their households and held garage sales, with the proceeds supporting the Christmas Miracle Offering. Families have spent less on each other so they could give more. Some accepted the challenge to fast through lunch each day, saving the money they would have spent on that meal to donate to the project.

The children's ministry has hosted the Sudan Bazaar for the last nine years. This is a one-day sale where children and families can host a booth to sell handmade, homemade goods, and all of the profits go to the Sudan Project. Families have made hot cocoa mixes, baked goods, candy, ornaments, dog treats, jewelry, and the list goes on. Children have sung and played instruments. Local businesses have donated goods and services to the silent auction portion of the bazaar. All of this has been to raise money to help the people in a country most have forgotten.

A few years into the project, Ginghamsburg changed things up by starting the campaign for the Miracle Offering with Christmas in July. "Giving calendars" that laid out a plan of weekly giving were given out to the congregation. Whether the goal for an individual or family was five hundred dollars or five thousand dollars, the calendars helped people to start planning for their contributions to the Miracle Offering in advance.

People connected with the need. They looked beyond themselves and their own comfort, and reached deep into their pockets to help these people across the globe. They became more aware of the situation, researching and learning on their own. They connected with Sudanese refugees in their own city of Dayton. Parents taught their children about generosity with the message of the struggle of the Sudanese people and the Christmas Miracle Offering.

Despite the phenomenal, ongoing success Ginghamsburg had with the Sudan Project, the church eventually had to deal with the reality that any congregation can have a short attention span. Whether it is because people became fatigued with denying their own desires, tired of hearing the same message, or disappointed that their sacrifice didn't effect change more quickly, the vision of the Christmas Miracle Offering began to lack the same force. A church that wants to continue its work has to keep the message fresh, paint pictures of positive change, and stay receptive to shifting the focus to the areas that will elicit a response from the congregation.

One question Ginghamsburg Church began asking itself, especially after it added campuses in downtown Dayton, was, "What about the people in need in our own community?" In response to this sentiment, the congregation began to include a few vital local ministries as beneficiaries of the Miracle Offering. Joshua Recovery House helps newly released inmates transition back into society with financial education, sobriety, and spiritual growth. Two new branches of the New Creation Counseling Center offer affordable Christian counseling to members of the community. Expanded GED programs at Ginghamsburg's Fort McKinley campus in Dayton educate and empower those without a high school diploma. And Fort McKinley's Food Pantry was equipped to provide fresh food for clients.

Adding a focus on local ministries in Dayton that served the nearby community revitalized Ginghamsburg's Christmas Miracle Offering. In hindsight, it is understandable that the congregations at Fort McKinley and The Point, whose campuses were located in lower-income neighborhoods, had trouble catching the passion for the Sudan Project and did not embrace the African Christmas design of Ginghamsburg's Advent sermon series. Incorporating local ministries that meet local needs made the Christmas Miracle Offering something all of the Ginghamsburg campuses could get behind.

Another way Ginghamsburg raises funds is by staying connected to its faithful givers. Twice annually they hold "Kingdom Investor" dinners to keep givers up-to-date on the health of the church. This is an opportunity to give updates on the vision and direction of the church, including statistics about the previous Christmas Miracle Offering, church plants, attendance, and the church's financial health. At times, this has been as detailed as charts and graphs showing how much Ginghamsburg spends on staffing, missions, building, and operating costs. Other times, it has taken the shape of an intimate discussion about building programs or campus expansions.

Apart from these semiannual dinners, Ginghamsburg reaches out to regular givers when times get tough. In Ohio, the weather can play a major role in cash flow through the offering plate. In the first six weeks of 2014, it snowed one or both days of every weekend. The church knows that most giving occurs when the basket is passed down the row on weekends, yet even the mere perception of bad weather can keep families at home. Plus, families rarely make up that missed giving opportunity the following weekend. When too many of these weekends come consecutively, the habit of giving can be broken. Meanwhile, when the weather truly is bad, there is the additional expense of plowing multiple driveways and parking lots.

As a consequence, very early in the year, Ginghamsburg found itself significantly behind budget, so they sent a letter to faithful givers to explain the situation and encourage them to make up any giving opportunities they might have missed. Those who had continued to give through this time were asked to give a little extra. The church included an envelope labeled "snow offering" that could be dropped into the plate or mailed to the church.

Even more recently, Ginghamsburg found itself in a tight financial spot unrelated to the weather. Some families had moved, and many empty nesters had become more irregular in their attendance. While the church continued to attract young families, these families are typically not in a life stage to be big givers, as twentysomethings are often carrying the burden of student loans, mortgages, car payments, and credit card debt. Again, Ginghamsburg sent a letter simply stating the need. They were honest with those they serve by letting them know that if they did not make up the deficit in the budget, staff could be affected.

It's never easy to ask for money, especially from those who have already demonstrated financial faithfulness. However, when church leaders are transparent with their congregation and build the relationship with them, many will respond. If individuals support the church and believe it is managing its resources well, many will step up and sacrifice more to support the mission.

Ginghamsburg also takes the financial health of its congregation seriously. Each fall, the church gives a four-week sermon series on stewardship that wraps up by asking the congregation to make a pledge to support the church for the next year. The teaching during these weeks is focused on biblical stewardship; practical teaching on debt, giving, and saving; and a word of caution about recognizing the difference between needs and wants and living beyond one's financial means.

This is also the time the church opens registration for the winter classes on money such as Financial Peace University and The Legacy Journey. (These classes are offered three times each year, but many are encouraged to take action during the stewardship series.) The church also offers one-meeting classes on retirement, saving for college, home buying, and how to get out of debt.

It is the church's intention to provide practical resources to equip families to achieve financial health and freedom. A congregation full of people enslaved by debt will never reach its full potential to impact its community or the world. A compelling vision will not only help motivate people to be engaged in generosity but will, hopefully, encourage people to be debt free and engaged in mission.

Chapter 3

USING YOUR ASSETS

One of the great responsibilities that I have is to manage my assets wisely, so that they create value.

—*Alice Walton*

One of his disciples, Andrew, Simon Peter's brother, said, "A youth here has five barley loaves and two fish. But what good is that for a crowd like this?" (John 6:8-9)

Many churches look to the offering plate or church fundraisers that bring in small sums in order to support the ministries of the church. However, pastors and leaders should refocus on other potential assets like land, buildings, and items in storage that can fund the mission, generate revenue, and create outreach opportunities for the church.

Wesley and His Instruction on Church Buildings

John Wesley, the founder of Methodism, once declared, "The world is my parish." He was a pastor and itinerant field preacher whose passion focused on the conversion of people and spiritual growth of followers of Jesus Christ. Wesley preached his first sermon in a brickyard, reaching out where people were.

Although Wesley primarily preached where the people were, his movement grew, eventually necessitating buildings. His first building, The New Room, in Bristol, England, was built with a simple design so it would be accessible to the common people of the area.[1] Wesley left instructions on church buildings in his work *The Nature, Design, and General Rules of the United Societies*. Wesley stated,

> Let all our Chapels be built plain and decent but not more expensively than is absolutely unavoidable: Otherwise, the necessity of raising money will make rich men necessary for us. But if we must be dependent upon them, yea, and governed by them, and then farewell to the Methodist Discipline, if not doctrine too.[2]

Wesley wanted church buildings to be simple and functional, rather than extravagant.

In this chapter, we'll look at several ways churches can use their buildings and other assets to maximize functionality. Sometimes an old building is a beautiful, sacred, functioning space for the community it serves, worthy of preservation while it continues to house and serve its congregation and others. Other times a church has become quiet because, in an attempt to preserve an old building, some have forgotten that the goal is to receive and host as many people as possible. Embrace Church's story is particularly inspiring in the ways it handed its assets to God and repurposed them so that God would multiply God's provisions to the community.

The Time Some Old Handbells Were the Fish and the Loaves

The reality show *Hoarders* examines the disease many people have of amassing possessions regardless of their value (or lack of it). Hoarders typically have an exaggerated sense that they will someday need all of that junk, and therefore cannot bring themselves to part with it. The results are heaps of useless possessions, anxiety about decisions related to possessions, a constant need for new space in which to hold or organize all their possessions, dysfunctional spaces in which to live and work, and an irrational compulsion to protect their junk from would-be thieves (or cleaners!).

I'd like to suggest that the local church struggles with hoarding on an organizational level. Sometimes items are kept out of a sense of thriftiness. Other times they are kept out of a sense of nostalgia or reverence for church history. These are legitimate feelings. However, like a house that needs to be cleaned out and reordered once or twice a year in order to stay congruous to the dynamics of human life, a church that wants to better utilize its spaces must clean house. Often, a church keeps things just because it doesn't know what it has. Some churches haven't had a workday in years and don't have a clue what they have in storage. Every few years, a local church can rent out a Dumpster or gather items for a rummage sale, thereby maximizing and repurposing space for ministry.

Without seed money to restart the Epworth campus (the campus Embrace merged with), I had to break a few rules to survive. Desperate times called for desperate measures. Knowing that the bills were mounting up while trying to restart a young church plant, I decided to inventory all of the church's assets, namely the property they owned. As I did so, I came across some old silver handbells. I didn't realize the value of silver at the time, but a friend shared how valuable the handbells were. I didn't believe him, so I googled it. I was shocked to learn that the going rate was about five thousand dollars for a set—and we had two sets! There was no question we had to sell the bells. They had been stashed away in the balcony, and the church's handbell choir had ceased to exist twenty years prior, so I knew nobody was going to miss them. I listed both sets on Craigslist, and a traditional church in Kentucky bought them for eight thousand dollars. When someone arrived to pick up the handbells, I have to admit I met them in the back parking lot because I didn't want anybody to see me carrying them out the front doors of the church; I felt as though I was transacting a drug deal! No, I didn't ask for permission to do it, nor did I call a meeting about it, but when my finance team received the check, they were happy. God provided badly needed cash through some handbells—handbells that would never be an asset to our church the way they would be to their new owners. (And, in case you're wondering, over the next few years at the church, not one person inquired about those missing handbells.)

When consulting with pastors who are strapped for cash and working to restart, I often ask them about their assets and mention the handbells. Many chuckle at the story. One pastor took my advice literally and sold his church's handbells for ten thousand dollars, revenue that funded his church's music ministry for well over a year!

Not every church has sets of old silver handbells lying around. But many churches do have items that have been collecting dust ever since the church moved on to a new way of doing things. Plus, assets like handbells are a lot easier to liquidate than real property. Yes, it may sound silly to say, "Have a garage sale!" but have you inventoried your physical assets lately? Online sites make selling items easier than ever, and, at the very least, you'll end up with some extra space.

Worthless Property and Arlington Studios

After the smaller items are inventoried, appraised, and potentially sold, congregations must turn their focus to their real property. Just because a property or a building has belonged to a faith community for as long as anyone can remember does not automatically justify its continued use and ownership by the church. In fact, the country is in a period of great potential for thousands of congregations to reconsider their land and building use. In the 1950s, thousands of churches were built across the country in areas that were considered solidly middle to upper middle class. These churches were large, beautiful, and traditional in design. Built in the days of low energy costs, they were also not very efficient with space or energy. But in the decades to follow, the country experienced the rapid growth of energy costs combined with the phenomenon of urban flight. Thousands of church buildings, once flagships of their denominations, have become very costly to maintain and heat. Urban flight has left the congregations that meet in those buildings with a declining giving base that is increasingly unable to pay for those buildings' expenses.

Worse yet, traditional faith communities, as they struggle to stay alive, often attempt to balance their budgets by deferring maintenance—thereby piling up expenses for future generations of churchgoers. Many of these buildings are in need of serious repair and updates, but the size and financial strength of the corresponding congregations are inadequate to the task. This vicious cycle has led congregations to close down ministries and sell their properties to whomever they can. Many congregations are left to choose between costly relocations or the complete dissolution of their churches. Also, the heating and cooling of aging church buildings are not cost effective if they are only used for the

37

congregation itself. Over the years studies conducted by New Beginnings Assessment Service found that many Disciples of Christ, United Church of Christ, and Presbyterian congregations struggle with their buildings revealing

> on average, a church is using only about 32 percent of the space they have available on a given Sunday. These same congregations use only about 25 percent of their sanctuary seating capacity and are spending more than a third of their budgets on heating and cooling all of their space—most of which is not used.[3]

Embrace Church's Arlington Project is an example of a highly desirable, viable option in the face of this reality. Embrace is located in an area affected by the circumstances just described. Embrace had a beautiful church building, solidly built, but in need of updates and maintenance. It also had a dilapidated parsonage, a large space of empty asphalt, and an empty grass lot that had been purchased thirty years earlier in hopes that the church would grow and need additional parking space.

That never happened. What did happen is that these unused lots gained notoriety because anytime there was a heavy downpour, the adjacent streets turned into "Lake Loudon" and "Lake Limestone" due to inadequate drainage from the lots. Meanwhile, Embrace lacked the finances to upgrade our outdated, struggling physical structure.

The trustees spoke about selling off the vacant asphalt lot. Mistakes were made along the way in getting that lot sold, but eventually we had all the approval and buy-in necessary to contact a real estate agent and get a "for sale" sign out on the lot. Little did we know that one inquiry on the land would turn into a miracle in front of our eyes.

The inquiry had come from a local developer, Bruce Nicol, who articulated his vision for the land as a housing project. Nicol didn't have high-end condos in mind, but rather something similar to a project he had completed with another family-owned property called Northridge Apartments. At Northridge Apartments, Nicol had made a unique arrangement with the Chrysalis House, a non-profit recovery program for women. At the housing project he envisioned on our lots, Nicol was willing to take a risk on a potential tenant, someone who may struggle to qualify for an apartment elsewhere, if the church or the Chrysalis House had a relationship with the individual. The two passions came together in a program that allows Chrysalis House graduates the chance to sublet an apartment through the recovery program until they can support themselves.

When I heard the developer's passion for providing affordable housing to people in need, I told him that the church had even more land it wasn't using. At the mention of the possibility, his eyes lit up, and a partnership started through which we were able to vision together the role Embrace could play in walking alongside the residents of the housing development.

Furthermore, this project would meet the needs of a community undergoing gentrification. The need in the North Limestone area of Lexington for secure, up-to-date, affordable housing had been well documented. The complex, which opened its doors summer of 2016, offers eighty micro-unit apartments with the bottom floor of each building designated for commercial use, such as laundry services, restaurants, or coffee shops. The three-hundred- to five-hundred-square-foot units are open to all, likely appealing to people from a mixed socio-economic background. The target tenants are individuals or couples who make between twenty thousand and forty thousand dollars a year, with each unit priced between four hundred and seven hundred dollars a month, utilities included.

The six-million-dollar complex—consisting of two buildings, one on each side of Embrace Church—has been dubbed "Lexington's most innovative housing project." The studios provide secure housing close to the city center, at fixed rates including rent and utilities, are built to satisfy LEED certification standards to minimize their environmental footprint, and are built with high-quality materials to encourage a sense of community pride and stewardship.

There were many other positive factors as well. Once the land deal closed and ownership transferred, Embrace had no financial or management obligations relating to the development. Additionally, the project included resolution of local storm water problems relating to the church and broader community, as identified in a grant awarded to Embrace by the city, for which the project developer became the subcontractor for the grant.

The sale value ended up at $390,000, consisting of $265,000 in cash and an increase in the value of property retained by Embrace of $125,000 (resulting from a zoning change). In the meantime, Embrace had no obligations related to the cost of architectural design, storm water design, marketing materials, or zone-change related fees.

Embrace had said, "Our community is hungry for ministry. We do not have the financial security to feed our community. What we do have is this empty, unused, drainage-mess of a lot." Although the unused property seemed to be of little value in the face of our growing needs as a church, God ultimately multiplied it in amazing, unforeseen ways. Embrace received needed revenues and fiscal stability. The purchaser received a lot on which to fulfill a vision of helping others while operating successfully as a business. Many low-income earners will receive affordable housing where there was none before. And, most importantly, Embrace will receive significant ongoing outreach opportunities in the community that will develop around it, presenting an ideal demographic for reconstituting a healthy and growing ministry base.[4]

The choice to be entrepreneurial and to take risks can oftentimes leave churches uneasy. However, when desperation sets in or, more importantly, when there is a burden for a local community, the potential reward outweighs the risk for churches to become a blessing to their community rather than a gatekeeper to a church building. Like many other churches, Embrace made the decision to fulfill the words of the prophet in Isaiah 61:4: "They will *rebuild* the ancient ruins; they will *restore* formerly deserted places; they will *renew* ruined cities, places deserted in generations past" (emphasis added).

What would it look like if local churches turned toward rebuilding, restoring, and renewing their communities rather than maintaining a "fortress" mentality about preserving their institutional buildings and keepsakes, keeping the carpet clean, and trying to control the noise volume? This shift could result in state-of-the-art housing, attention paid to persons with income substantially below the local median, community partnerships, and a breath of life for struggling urban faith communities.

Parsonages

Another underutilized resource common to many local churches is the parsonage. Originally, parsonages housed pastors and their families. However, many pastors today are given a housing allowance instead, which provides them the freedom to choose where they want to live and helps them build equity in their own home. Today, few parsonages actually still house pastors. Nevertheless, it's not out of the ordinary for churches to own more than one parsonage. Some churches may even own up to three or four homes, often as the result of parishioners dying and passing on their property to their local church.

The parsonage belonging to Embrace Church was sitting empty. Instead of viewing it as a liability, the church decided to figure out how it could be a resource. The congregation didn't have enough money to make improvements to the parsonage that would be required to rent it out for income. On the other hand, it was a suitable place to use as a way to compensate a few junior, single staff members. It therefore became known as a perpetual bachelor pad. Embrace's custodian and Gathering service pastor were roommates who lived in the parsonage for three years while they served at Embrace. Then, when one left, someone else moved in. It became a sort of mission house as well. It was a place that urban missionaries, staff members, and people who needed a place to stay could call home in exchange for much-needed labor and help at the church.

Since the parsonage was adjacent to the church and the backyard was not used, this became the perfect location for a community garden. Children and youth learned valuable lessons in gardening, observing plants grow, and harvesting them. The community garden was also the source of many of the salads consumed at Embrace's community meals. The garden contained a variety of vegetables: tomatoes, peppers, cucumbers, and beans. Church leaders harvested vegetables and distributed them to neighbors. Community members were encouraged to harvest and use the vegetables themselves.

When an urban community is defined as a food desert, with restricted access to fresh, healthy vegetables and other foods, free green spaces should be used to reestablish access to healthy foods and the experience of gardening.

> The Lord God proclaims: On the day that I cleanse you of all your guilt, I will cause the cities to be inhabited, and the ruins will be rebuilt. The desolate land will be farmed, and it won't be like it was when it seemed a wasteland to all who passed by. They will

say, "This land, which was a desolation, has become like the garden of Eden." And the cities that were ruined, ravaged, and razed are now fortified and inhabited. The surviving nations around you will know that I, the LORD, have rebuilt what was torn down and have planted what was made desolate. I, the LORD, have spoken, and I will do it. (Ezek 36:33-36)

Creative Ways Churches Use Space throughout the Country

When Embrace merged with the Epworth campus, which was built in 1950, it cleaned out a room next to the sanctuary. The room had not been touched in years because it was the choir room—and since the church hadn't had a choir in twenty years, it was better known as storage space for any piece of furniture or box of supplies that someone didn't know what to do with. In order to move forward with a new vision for the space, the new pastor and staff first paid tribute to the sacrifice of the older members.

Many of the elderly members can remember the sacrifice that went into building the facility. The fund-raising and construction of the building resembled something out of the book of Acts when, for the sake of the kingdom, many sold possessions, remortgaged their homes, and worked overtime to save extra money to literally buy each brick for the building. One member of seventy-two years, who has lived in the same house near the church for close to fifty years, recalled how she and her family would walk to church and prayer services in order to open parking spaces for other families who had to travel a distance to church. She believes the church building built on North Limestone brought the congregation closer together because it was a task that everybody had to participate in to make happen. God provided for Epworth one step at a time, brick by brick.

That faithfulness was lifted up in sermons and in meetings so that the heritage could be honored while a new vision of turning the choir room into a community café was being pursued. Pictures from the glory days of the Epworth faithful were hung in a corner of the hallway that had been made into a small heritage space. Of course, there were a few old-timers who were naysayers at the beginning of the project. They were given the opportunity to take any items in the room that held sentimental value. (No matter how well a vision is communicated, there will always be a few who don't want to catch it and who will stand opposed to it. Usually they are few in number, but loud.)

Nevertheless, the space was totally transformed and made useful. A local Christian businessman who didn't even attend Embrace caught the vision and decided to donate all of the materials and labor for the new café. Local artists displayed their art on the walls, and musicians were welcomed to play at open-mic nights.

One church that has found creative uses for its extra space is Austin Stone Community Church in Austin, Texas. One of the church's campuses is a former retirement home that was converted into a state-of-the-art facility. Worship services are held there on Sunday, and various nonprofits use the space for their offices during the week.

In the Kensington neighborhood of Philadelphia, Beacon is a faith community that offers free after-school creative classes for neighborhood children. The church is committed to serving as a creative space and community center. The Studio, its free after-school program, offers classes in writing, story-sharing, and visual art. The children's artwork covers the walls of the church sanctuary, and the basement where the classes meet is stuffed with arts and crafts supplies. Former art teachers and residents from the neighborhood serve as volunteers for the program.[5]

There are numerous other examples of churches creatively using their spaces to reach their communities. Some faith communities allow Boy and Girl Scouts, Weight Watchers, Alcoholics Anonymous, Al-Anon, GriefShare, cancer support groups, sports leagues, and other programs to use their spaces during the week. There are others who allow local public schools to rent an entire wing for ESL and GED classes.

Another creative way a church can use its building is to become a co-working space. Regarded by some as the future of work, co-working is a style of work that involves a shared working environment, but independent activity. People who work in a co-working space are usually not employed by the same organization, nor are they necessarily in the same profession. What if the church building was a place where entrepreneurs, business leaders, city officials, and others routinely meet and work?

In Brooklyn, New York, a church decided to become a co-working space in its community. St. Lydia's opened the space, helping to make the congregation financially sustainable. In fact, this venture allowed the church to establish itself in a permanent location, no longer forced to move from place to place because they lacked sufficient funds to settle in one building.[6]

A once-dying church in Detroit's Eastern Market area is experiencing new life thanks to a space-sharing agreement between the church and two local performing arts groups. St. John-St. Luke Evangelical United Church of Christ allowed ArtLab J, a fledgling contemporary dance company, and the Young Fenix Physical Theatre, the United Church of Christ's performing arts outreach program, to move into its space. The arts groups have an affordable space to work, while the church benefits from the new people and finances coming through its doors.[7]

A new church plant in San Pedro, Colorado, The Garden Church, is "re-imagining church as an interconnected organism, worshipping, loving, and serving together as they transform a plot of land into a vibrant urban garden."[8] Instead of worshipping in a building, they leased a lot in the heart of San Pedro where they created a pop-up garden and gathering space for worship. Currently, the faith community is in its third phase of its church planting strategy: planting an edible urban sanctuary to welcome people for physical and spiritual nourishment.

How many times have you driven by a church building during the week and seen an empty parking lot? The pastor and some staff may be there, but the actual building remains largely unused throughout the week. A goldmine of opportunity is within the church's reach, but one must have eyes to see in order to notice it. A church's property is one of the greatest assets it has for its community. One way churches can use the resources in front of them is to creatively use their space.

When brainstorming possible uses for your real estate, it is important to ask yourself open-ended questions: How is God's kingdom calling you to consider new and creative ways to use your physical space? Is there a ministry in your community that needs a new home? Is there a way to meet some need in your community by giving some space away? After contemplating those questions, take an assessment of your physical space throughout the church building. Possible spaces include classrooms, meeting rooms, kitchens, sanctuaries, parking lots, courtyard/garden, choir room, stage, and storage areas.[9]

Additionally, spring-cleaning can prevent clutter and allow a church to more readily assess when a space is due for repurposing.

There are a few people in every church with a passion not only for tidying up but also for sorting, purging, and creating lasting systems of organization. A workday every year or two can achieve these goals and, in the process, build community as people work together, remembering what items were used for in the past, dreaming about their usefulness in the future, and brainstorming ways to clean up.

Classrooms

Most churches have classrooms used for Bible studies and Sunday school on weekends, but they sit empty during the week. What if those empty classrooms could be used during the week to host GED classes? ESL classes? Parenting classes? Those classrooms may be the perfect space for a book club to meet or just what a local music teacher needs for giving lessons.

Meeting Rooms

Many churches have a large meeting space used for occasional events and receptions. Why not let a local study group book it for a lecture? Why not allow families to use it for birthday parties? Would a small coffeehouse be perfect for the space at least once per week?

Kitchens

Licensed commercial kitchens can be hard to find for young caterers or others just starting out in the food business, but most churches have one. This is the perfect space to offer for rental during the week.

Sanctuary

Sanctuaries provide a place where a large group of people can come together at once. What if your sanctuary could be used for neighborhood meetings with elected officials, or as a place where community members could come discuss and find solutions to problems that plague the neighborhood?

Parking Lots

Especially in an urban area where parking spaces are scarce, opening a parking lot during unused hours can be a draw for potential renters. There are a number of ways the arrangement could be made, whether it's charging a monthly fee to individual tenants for weeknight parking or renting it to groups for parking during specific events.

Courtyard/Garden

An outdoor courtyard or garden can serve as a venue for parties, weddings, or other outdoor events.

Choir Room

The organ and choir setup in many churches can be a great space for musicians who need to practice. The acoustics in a church are often excellent, hard to replicate, and exactly what a musician in your community needs. Consider offering this space as a music rehearsal space for organists, pianists, and other choirs.

Stage

Many churches have a stage, perhaps used only a few times a year for school plays or a Christmas pageant. Many towns have theater groups looking for an affordable place to stage performances. A stage could also serve as a venue for dance rehearsals or photo shoots for an aspiring photographer.

Storage Areas

Churches with a lot of buildings may have unused storage spaces—closets in basements, outdoor sheds or garages, and so forth. These, too, can be made available to renters. They might be just what a Little League team needs to store their equipment in the off-season, or what a young entrepreneur needs for inventory storage.

What spaces do you need to reclaim in your local church to make room for ministry to happen? What can be repurposed for the church or the community? Stewardship includes the care of buildings that have been entrusted to local congregations. Just because a building is large, old, and less energy-efficient than modern buildings doesn't automatically make it a liability. On the other hand, if church buildings are treated like museums where people feel as if they can't touch anything, they will not feel welcome. These buildings can be turned into assets simply by getting rid of what is useless and making room for the new thing God wants to do in the space. Jesus speaks to this in Matthew 9:17: "No one pours new wine into old wineskins. If they did, the wineskins would burst, the wine would spill, and the wineskins would be ruined. Instead, people pour new wine into new wineskins so that both are kept safe." Church buildings can be a blessing not only for the local church and their members but also for the surrounding community as "new wineskins": meeting spaces, rehearsal and concert halls, workspaces, areas for art exhibits, and a whole host of innovative purposes that could bring more foot traffic to the building.

Chapter 4

PARTNERS

If you can dream it up, you can team it up.

—Richie Norton

He directed the disciples to seat all the people in groups as though they were having a banquet on the green grass. They sat down in groups of hundreds and fifties. He took the five loaves and the two fish, looked up to heaven, blessed them, broke the loaves into pieces, and gave them to his disciples to set before the people. He also divided the two fish among them all. (Mark 6:39-41)

Often our best assets take the shape of partnerships with other people and groups. When two groups, sometimes even unlikely pairs, come together to work on a mutual vision, amazing things can happen. We call this synergy: the multiplication of impact beyond the known sum of each group's individual strengths.

A church can be guilty of trying to reinvent the wheel or trying to do things by themselves, their way. But effective ministry looks to other churches, nonprofits, community leaders, businesses, and even the local government for possible partnerships. This saves resources and can multiply the influence of a church, so long as the partnerships line up with vision and mission.

When Embrace Church says that everything they learned about shared community space and resources came from a microbrewery, people think they're joking. Yet microbreweries have become hugely successful in cities across the country in the past three decades, in part because they have become champions of the neolocalist movement to reestablish and reinforce community ties. West Sixth Brewery in Lexington is no exception.

The unique thing about West Sixth Brewery in Lexington (other than being sued by Magic Hat over a logo infringement claim) is that it shares its enormous facility with dynamic partners who help further their mission in the community. West Sixth Brewery's location is in a once-abandoned building from the 1890s known as the Bread Box because it was formerly home to the Rainbow Bread Bakery for over a century. When the founders of West Sixth Brewery "bought the Bread Box building and started West Sixth Brewery nearly four years ago, they said they wanted to do more than make money and good beer. They wanted to make their community a better place to live."[1] This is evidenced by the ten partners that occupy the ninety-thousand-square-foot facility. The partners include Broke Spoke Community Bike Shop (a nonprofit community bicycle shop), the Rollergirls of Central Kentucky (roller derby), the Plantory (an innovative and energizing co-working hub that fosters collaboration and nurtures growth for positive, passionate, and community-minded businesses and nonprofit organizations), the Bread Box Studio Artists (creative professionals working in a communal art space, ranging from authors to photographers, to printmakers, mixed-media artists, textile artists, and more), Food Chain (an urban agriculture nonprofit), Smithtown Seafood (Lexington's newest farm-to-table restaurant where everything on the menu is made from scratch, and whenever possible, with locally raised ingredients), Bluegrass

Distillers, Magic Beans Coffee Roasters, and Cricket Press (a design and poster-printing operation).

West Sixth Brewery gives back to the community in other ways too. "The partners donate 6 percent of profits to charity, plus make other donations and host monthly fundraisers where a different nonprofit group receives 6 percent of sales. Last year, the company's giving totaled about $100,000, partner Ben Self said."[2] Arguably, this microbrewery is making more of an impact than several local churches in their community. They believe in partnership. They utilize to their advantage a ninety-thousand-square-foot facility that many would consider a liability. They host fundraisers for causes that are important to their community. They give money back where they live. They have become a center for innovation and entrepreneurship. They are clear and concise with their vision, mission, and values.

Another aspect of West Sixth Brewery's philosophy worth replicating is that they choose their partnerships strategically. Not every opportunity to partner makes sense for their vision. They know exactly what they want to accomplish and are unapologetic about it. As Embrace Church sought to be an anchor in their community, they wanted to throw their doors wide open, but they also learned to not chase every opportunity. Working with groups that had common interests prevented them from being spread too thin. If local churches have not yet zeroed in on the specific vision God has for their communities, or if they have trouble staying focused on what God has uniquely called them to be and do in their community, then this model of partnership will look different and should not be reproduced in their facility. Without a clear identity, involving more partners will only muddy the waters for the local church and the community they are trying to reach out to serve.

Embrace Church's Strategic Partners

Root 12

The possibility of the Arlington Studio apartments birthed an idea for another nonprofit out of Embrace Church called Root 12. In spite of the overwhelming number of great social service organizations in Lexington and throughout major cities in the U.S., a large percentage of the disadvantaged population has not yet found the means or methods necessary to live a purposeful and self-supported life. Former executive pastor LeTicia Preacely began Root 12 to address this problem. The mission is straight-forward: Root 12 engages in individual elevation by providing transformative instruction and assisting with life-stabilizing needs through key partnerships. Root 12 serves the underprivileged by helping people discover their purpose and increase self-sustainability, gainful employment, and stable housing through life coaching, mentoring, spiritual guidance, partnerships, and community engagement. Root 12 also empowers people, especially those on the margins, to have a transformative impact on social justice issues within our community.

The organization's name refers both to its mission and to its method. By definition, a root is an anchoring organ, pulling sustenance from a plant's environs, enabling the plant to carry on its necessary life processes, all while contributing to surrounding soil health. The twelve is based on Jesus Christ's model of doing life with twelve individuals who accept an invitation to be a student of life. They believe Jesus's approach of mutual dedication among a few while serving all who seek assistance is the catalytic formula for community empowerment and transformation. Root 12 helps as many people as possible while doing life with twelve committed Life Scholars each year.

One example of how Root 12 contributes to the health of its community is by providing data collected through surveys, interviews, and other research to its partner organizations, so that they can improve their own services. As individuals and organizations become stronger, and the people work to address social justice issues at a grassroots level, systemic injustices in our communities will diminish. Root 12 also works with "at risk" youth in much the same way to increase the success rate of this group as they become adults.

From January through December, each Life Scholar receives individual mentorship, guidance, and training from the executive director and a team of professionals who specialize in different areas. A "Customized Life Plan" (CLP) is developed for each person that ensures Root 12 is meeting the individual's needs throughout the year. From a programming standpoint, instruction focuses on advocacy skills, social awareness, workforce enhancement, personal development, and entrepreneurship. The program includes individual sessions, small group workshops, training sessions, and joint large-group sessions. As a part of the twelve-month intensive partnership, each Life Scholar is guided through selecting a social justice issue in the community and creating a strategic plan to significantly impact this area throughout the year. Spiritual guidance and purpose discovery is also a crucial service that is provided to each Life Scholar throughout this process. As a group, prayer and Bible-based devotionals are incorporated into workshops, trainings, and other aspects of programming.

Root 12's mission is directly aligned with the mission of Embrace Church, and it has therefore been a perfect opportunity for partnership. Embrace is able to share in the missional harvest that results from Root 12's outreach, all while sharing the costs associated with the endeavor.

Common Good

Another primary partner of Embrace Church is Common Good. Common Good is an after-school program that serves youth in kindergarten through twelfth grade four days a week during both the school year and summer. The kids receive a nutritious meal each day, a safe place to be during after-school hours and during the summer, increased accountability in completing homework and making good grades, the opportunity to form positive bonds with adult mentors, and a chance to hang out with peers in a supervised environment.

Common Good has an interesting genesis. Area youth were already being served by a growing ministry. While the kids' spiritual needs were being met, they still needed transformation in their academic performance and family lives. Common Good was born out of this desire to reach out beyond the typical Wednesday evening and Sunday morning youth ministry programming.

There are fifty spots for students in Common Good. Common Good targets three strategic neighborhoods around Embrace Church: North Limestone, Castlewood, and East End. The church allows Common Good to meet in their basement rent-free and encourages their laity to serve in the ministry, as they are able. This allows Embrace to serve members of the community and build relationships with neighbors who may not otherwise come to the church. Common Good also draws from other churches and organizations to fill the thirty-five weekly volunteer mentor positions. Mentors commit to volunteering one day a week for a school semester or summer. They tutor, encourage, challenge, and otherwise build relationships with students.

For many of Common Good's students, the summertime months lack structure. Child care is prohibitively expensive for the families Common Good serves. Furthermore, few enrichment opportunities for children and youth exist due to transportation issues, budget cuts for summer programming, and program restrictions. From the students' perspectives, summer is boring with so little going on. Some students have little to no supervision during the summer, and the temptation to get into trouble increases. This is where Common Good's program stepped in to meet another basic need. In the summer, the group organizes activities that focus on leadership development, recreation, and spiritual formation. The middle school and high school students go on college visits to begin learning about the process, understanding the grades they need to earn in order to attend college, and finding out what scholarship opportunities exist. Many of these students are first-generation Latinos and African refugees, and most will be the first in their families to attend college. In the spring of 2015, all four graduating seniors involved in Common Good completed high school and were accepted into college for the fall. Common Good walked these students and their families through the application process and helped them locate and pursue scholarship opportunities.

In its first three years, the volunteer mentors, paid staff, and community members involved in Common Good have impacted a few hundred students. The 501(c)(3) began as a dream and now has full-time staff and a budget that sustains the ministry's growth. Common Good has molded students into not only disciples of Jesus but also leaders. The scope and scale of Common Good surpassed the accomplishments of the traditional "youth group" model.

Common Good's vision is for our community to live into its God-given potential evidenced by thriving children, strong families, and flourishing neighborhoods, desiring that community members be reconciled to God and to each other. The neighborhoods that Common Good targets are under-resourced, and there is a well-known need for effective programming for children and youth in this area. The families in these neighborhoods face the harsh daily realities of living in poverty: single-parent homes; grandparents raising grandchildren; limited social support; the increasing presence of prostitution, drugs, and violence; and many also face the unique challenges of being immigrants and refugees. The odds are against many of these children and families, but there is hope.

El Sistema

While Common Good's after-school program operates in the basement of Embrace Church, an additional thirty elementary students meet on the second floor with another strategic partner, El Sistema.

El Sistema is an organization inspired by the famed Venezuelan classical music-education program founded in 1975 by musician and educator José Antonio Abreu. It is affiliated with Central Kentucky Youth Orchestra and Arlington Elementary School, which is directly across the street from Embrace Church.

This pilot program is one of several dozen across the nation that has become well known for equipping youngsters with musical skills, providing a safe haven after school, and shaping young leaders with a passion for the arts. El Sistema has gained traction at a time when public schools are experiencing drastic budget cuts to their arts programs. El Sistema is led by professionals who teach the concepts and philosophy of music for ninety minutes after school every day. They provide children in a low-income area with access to a phenomenal music education that out-performs many public school music programs. Through El Sistema, a student receives twelve hours of intensive music instruction each week, eliminating traditional access barriers by providing instruction and resources at no cost to participants in exchange for their full commitment to the program.

The benefits for Embrace Church were many. First, the church welcomes more children into an otherwise unused church space, which is an opportunity to interact with the parents who pick up their kids each day. It also provides rental income to help offset Embrace's yearly budgetary needs. There is an additional evangelistic opportunity to reach the community as hundreds of parents, teachers, and children would gather in the church sanctuary for performances during the school year. All this happened because Embrace was willing to use the main resource it had, which was not a ton of money or masses of church volunteers with whom to create their own programming, but simply their space.

The church quickly became known as a community center proactively investing in the life of the neighborhood. The goodwill shown to community residents and partners created relationships throughout the city of Lexington. The local church ought to be the safest and most hospitable place for people to come. When the church starts living into its role as host and caretaker, it begins to see evidence of the kingdom of God being built on earth little by little. It's impossible for one local church to do it all, but imagine if each church used exactly what it already had instead of allowing its perceived lack to define its actions.

UK Radio Station Concerts

Embrace was gaining a reputation throughout Lexington, not because of its huge budget, staff, or attendance, but because of its ability to take calculated risks and a willingness to be entre-preneurial. This gained attention from an unlikely place—the University of Kentucky radio station, WRFL. Throughout the school year, WRFL would host concerts for their students in various places in the city, culminating in their annual multi-venue event, Boomslang. In order to bring shows to the north side of Lexington, they decided to approach Embrace Church about participating in the festival. WRFL thought Embrace's Epworth campus would be a perfect location for multiple, simultaneous concerts in the sanctuary and the basement. Of course, Embrace was able to generate revenue from the rental agreement, but more importantly, it brought college students and local folks into the church who wouldn't otherwise have a reason to be there. WRFL was blown away by Embrace's hospitality and willingness to share their space, and this became a regular occurrence for many years. It was also a great way for the people of Embrace to give out free bottled waters and concessions to the students. It was a win-win for both groups.

Additionally, these concerts opened up the possibility for bands and musicians to use the church during the week for practice as a co-sharing space. It was a great way to connect with local artists and build inroads with the community. Groups pay a small fee and are able to access the facility during non-worship hours. The church has so much space, it even lets the musicians store their equipment in classrooms.

GleanKY and Seedleaf

As Embrace Church was discerning what a neighborhood garden would look like in their area, their vision was to build community while addressing the food desert that was staring them in the face. Food deserts are defined as parts of the country vapid of fresh fruit, vegetables, and other healthful whole foods, usually found in impoverished areas. This is largely due to a lack of grocery stores, farmers' markets, and healthy food providers. This has become a big problem because . . . they are heavy on local quickie marts that provide a wealth of processed, sugar, and fat laden foods that are known contributors to our nation's obesity epidemic.[3]

In Embrace's quest to provide a solution, they knew they couldn't do it alone, which is why they sought partnerships. The first partnership was with GleanKY, a nonprofit that gathers and redistributes excess fruits and vegetables to nourish Kentucky's hungry. GleanKY believes that gleaning fruits and vegetables that would otherwise go to waste is key to alleviating hunger and "food insecurity," which the USDA defines as a "limited or uncertain availability of nutritionally adequate and safe foods or limited or uncertain ability to acquire acceptable foods in socially acceptable ways."[4] They work with local farms, orchards, farmers' markets, grocery stores, supermarkets, and individual gardeners to provide hunger programs throughout central Kentucky with fresh, edible fruits and vegetables.

Gleaning is a biblical principle taken from the Old Testament in a directive given to Israel from God. Leviticus 19:9-10 says,

> When you harvest your land's produce, you must not harvest all the way to the edge of your field; and don't gather up every remaining bit of your harvest. Also do not pick your vineyard clean or gather up all the grapes that have fallen there. Leave these items for the poor and the immigrant; I am the LORD your God.

Embrace Church easily became a host site for fresh fruits and vegetables that were given to its community members and anybody who wanted them. This program did not cost Embrace anything. The church simply had to be willing to be a host site

61

for drop-offs that would take place once a week. The great thing about GleanKY is that the produce they glean is never sold and is only intended for food-insecure people, providing a link between local food sources and hunger programs such as the one Embrace was operating. GleanKY collects food more than eight hundred times a year with the ability to do more. These types of organizations exist in several cities but are lacking consistent partnerships. This could easily be an outreach program of any church that would not cost them a penny. The only resource required is volunteers willing to pass out the food.

Embrace Church also furthered its food programs in a partnership with Seedleaf. Seedleaf's mission is to nourish communities by growing, cooking, sharing, and recycling food. While GleanKY provides the food free of charge, Seedleaf empowers folks to grow their own food and, more importantly, teaches them how to cook it. Their philosophy is to start working with young people through the SEEDS program. SEEDS stands for Service, Education, and Entrepreneurship in Downtown Spaces and empowers youth in food deserts to stand for healthy food and make healthy lifestyle choices. After applying and being accepted, SEEDS kids meet twice each week during June and July for hands-on lessons and skills development in growing, cooking, sharing, and recycling food. With career development in mind, field trips and guest chefs add a taste of real-world opportunities to the regular tasks of cultivating and harvesting the garden.

The SEEDS program partnered with Common Good and gave the children in Embrace Church's neighborhood opportunities they otherwise would not have had. SEEDS gives kids a purpose in the summer: learning skills they'll use later in life, spending time outdoors and growing food, cooking and learning about culinary jobs, selling produce to neighbors, and making new friends—all while receiving a paycheck. SEEDS is a job. Youth who participate fully earn a graduation ceremony and receive a gift card for $250. But SEEDS is also a camp, with qualified leaders and volunteers who provide regular support and guidance to the youth. And SEEDS is fun—getting messy, whether in the garden or in the kitchen, is always a bonus.

After three years of SEEDS programming, the team is strong, experienced, and dedicated to creating a space of safety, respect, and lifelong memories. This was yet another program that cost Embrace nothing. The church simply helped recruit the kids and gave them an opportunity to be trained.

Lexington Rescue Mission

At the Monday night Gathering service, there were many who needed access to resources the church simply didn't have. That's where Lexington Rescue Mission (LRM) came in. They major in many of the resources Embrace minored in. When the opportunity arose for a resource counselor from LRM to take up office space at Embrace on Mondays, it became a referral service that complemented both organizations. Embrace doesn't have the budget to help people in financial crisis, but LRM does. It provides emergency financial assistance for rent and utility bills to families in crisis through its Homeless Prevention Program. When Embrace encountered individuals facing eviction or having their utilities shut off, it was able to connect them with one-on-one help, budget counseling, resource referral, and case management. In 2014 alone, LRM prevented eighty families from having utilities shut off and eighty-two households from being evicted.

Embrace also encountered many parishioners in need of substance abuse recovery. Many churches are not equipped to help people in recovery, but Embrace was fortunate to be able to connect folks to LRM's transitional housing, which is located a block from the church. LRM's recovery home, known as Potter's House, is geared toward men who have achieved at least thirty days of sobriety and have participated in a recovery program and need a safe place where they can practice those principles, be held accountable, and learn how to live a sober, healthy life. The residents are also required to attend a local church. Embrace would help nourish the spiritual needs of those individuals.

LRM was also an avenue for people to learn job skills, so Embrace Church encouraged their parishioners to participate in the Jobs for Life program, which trains people to find and maintain meaningful employment. The Jobs for Life program is an eight-week program designed from a faith perspective to help people grow in confidence and character as they receive support from the community. At the end of the eight weeks, there is a graduation ceremony that takes place at Embrace Church.

Providing space to the LRM counselor is almost like having an added church staff member that the church doesn't have to compensate because the circle of support is so complete. The counselors help job seekers find employment, assist tenants in obtaining affordable housing, help people navigate government programs (such as K-Tap and Social Security), and make referrals to important community resources.

LRM also runs a thrift store down the street from Embrace. This is the perfect avenue through which to provide clothing vouchers for individuals and families in need. They supply children and youth in need with new underwear, socks, pants, and shoes.

As if that wasn't enough, LRM helps Embrace's community with free medical care through their health clinic, which is open to residents without health insurance. It is staffed by a nurse practitioner and volunteer nurses and other medical professionals. In 2014, they provided more than four hundred free medical visits for the uninsured.

All of these resources came at no cost to Embrace Church other than the provision one day a week of an office that was previously unused. Typically churches have at least one empty office or are closed one weekday, making it easy to welcome in a trusted partner who aligns with a kingdom of God vision.

Because LRM and Embrace Church were willing to work together, they were able to fulfill Luke 4:18-19: "*The Spirit of the Lord is upon me, / because the Lord has anointed me. / He has sent me to preach good news to the poor, / to proclaim release to the prisoners / and recovery of sight to the blind, / to liberate the oppressed, / and to proclaim the year of the Lord's favor.*"

It was impossible for Embrace Church to meet all the needs of its community on their own. There was no reason for them to re-create the wheel, which is why they decided to partner with organizations that were in alignment with the church's mission to empower people. It's amazing when organizations can come together for the common good, bringing what they already have and seeing it multiplied right before their very eyes. Local churches see miracles every day—or are on the brink of miracles and don't recognize it. There is a pride in us and in our churches that says we can do it all on our own, according to our own ideas. But to operate out of this pride closes our access to powerful synergies that can develop out of purposeful partnerships.

Partnering Churches

Many urban churches find themselves in situations where it becomes difficult to reach out to their community because of financial barriers. However, when they are willing to work together, churches are enabled to give expansively to their communities. Unfortunately, it is somewhat unusual for churches to want to work together. The tendency, instead, is to be territorial and concerned about whose name is on the banner and where people attend church. Without partnerships with other churches, Embrace would not have been able to provide things like the Back to School Bash, backpack programs, community health fairs, Easter egg hunts, and numerous other services for the community.

Back to School Bash

Each year, the YMCA of Lexington provides backpacks full of school supplies for school-aged children at numerous sites if the sites are willing to provide games, activities, food, and volunteers for the day. Embrace has formed a partnership with Total Grace Baptist Church to provide the activities, food, and volunteers for the annual Back to School Rally in our Northside and Castlewood communities. The children and families are exceedingly blessed and get hyped about starting a new school year.

Backpack Program

Southern Hills United Methodist Church partnered with Embrace to provide a ministry to the students of Arlington Elementary who were on the free or reduced-cost lunch program, supplying food in backpacks for the family on weekends and during holiday breaks from school. Over 90 percent of the students who attend Arlington are on free or reduced lunch. Southern Hills UMC is located in a different part of Lexington where families tend to be more affluent, whereas Arlington Elementary is directly across the street from Embrace. It takes Southern Hills a few weeks to raise over thirty thousand dollars to provide the meals for the entire year. As a result, for some time, Southern Hills has used the space at Embrace to pack and store the food, bins, and backpacks that go to the families at Arlington. It is much easier to have volunteers assemble everything at Embrace and deliver it to the school from across the street than from across town. A lot of coordination goes into this ministry, so the calendar is agreed upon and set in advance. Then, a copy of the backpack schedule is always left on the food storage room door in the fellowship hall. The system that has developed is pretty efficient. All deliveries are made to Arlington by 9:30 a.m. on the last day of school for the week, according to the schedule on the door. The coordinator from Southern Hills communicates with the family resource person at Arlington Elementary to confirm the time and request the custodian's help with delivery if he is available. Then, a volunteer picks the storage bins up every Monday. During the pre-semester meeting, Embrace staff and the Southern Hills volunteer coordinator discuss the calendar and work around potential scheduling conflicts as much as possible. Overall, this partnership has been a blessing to both ministries and has worked to strengthen the relationship between the school and the church.

Easter Egg Hunt

In many low-income urban neighborhoods like North Limestone in Lexington, free events for the family are a big deal. One of the big community events Embrace had put on each year was an Easter egg hunt, which always drew a sizeable response from the community. This was an event Embrace loved to do, but it started to take a toll on the church's modest budget. Then, in 2013, the larger, more established Immanuel Baptist Church sought to partner with Embrace as a means of expanding their outreach efforts to a part of the community with a great need. As a result, this event was able to continue in the North Limestone corridor, albeit mostly funded by Immanuel. This event served hundreds in the community with games and activities, egg hunts for multiple age groups, a cookout, inflatables, live music, and a good time of fellowship. It was such a great use of space as well. The event took place inside the church, outside the building, and in the parking lot. An event such as this that required a great deal of organizing and coordination would not have happened without numerous volunteers from both churches.

Community Health Fair

In many urban areas children don't receive adequate health screenings. Embrace wanted to do something about it, and Immanuel Baptist Church decided to help. Embrace worked with Immanuel Baptist Church and Arlington Elementary to host a free wellness clinic for the community. More than two hundred volunteers offered services to nearly seventy families (more than two hundred people) from the community. The event featured medical, dental, and vision screenings as well as massages, kindergarten screenings, sports physicals, and immunizations, along with games for the kids, prayer, free snacks, Bibles, and information about healthy living. There was also a free lunch, cooked by professional chefs, in the fellowship hall of the Epworth campus church building. It was a great opportunity to partner with another church, let folks in the community know that Embrace cared for its neighbors, and offer services that many of the families in the community otherwise could not afford. Each family was also paired with an advocate who walked alongside them throughout the day and provided care for spiritual needs as requested.

Vital Church Mergers

The ultimate way a church can partner, especially when it is experiencing decline and can no longer maintain its space, is to become one entity with another church in a similar or complementary situation. Mergers may also occur when a larger church is seeking a location for a satellite church.[5] Many of the church mergers happening increasingly across the U.S. are producing positive growth and effective ministry to their communities, becoming agents for unifying local churches around a shared mission.[6]

If you drive down North Dixie Drive in Dayton, Ohio, you'll notice a stretch thick with signs for psychics and fortune readers and adult entertainment clubs—and local churches. One of these churches has a story similar to the stories of many mainline denominational churches. Once a vibrant church, Higher Ground United Methodist Church had faced decline for a variety of reasons in recent years. Worship attendance dropped to about forty people because many of its parishioners no longer lived in close proximity to the church, the average age of those churchgoers was seventy years old, and the congregation was predominantly white. In other words, those who did attend were not in the best position to serve their "local" community, as they were not representative of it, or even living in it.

In 2014, the church received a young supply pastor (a lay member appointed to serve a church) who was willing to take a risk in order to face the tall order of growing the congregation. Joshua Wynn knew that one of the ways to reach his new community was going to be through partnerships, especially given Higher Ground's limited resources, reduced staff, and lack of lay leadership. What Wynn couldn't anticipate was how far-reaching these partnerships would become.

Meanwhile, another local UMC called Residence Park had experienced a parallel decline. Residence Park was a nearby, predominantly African American congregation that had dwindled to twenty people. When pastor Daryl Williams entered the picture, the fact that the church's roof was literally caving in seemed an appropriate metaphor for the state of Residence Park as a whole. The original church building had become so dilapidated and neglected that the congregation was eventually forced to move out and meet in various places throughout the city. Williams describes that the congregation faced a desperate situation and that "the attachment to their church home was so profound that many members wanted to close rather than continue in another space—fortunately, that path was not chosen."[7]

At both Higher Ground and Residence Park, the challenges seemed insurmountable, but those challenges forced them to be innovative. A mutual colleague introduced Joshua Wynn and Daryl Williams. Both leaders had inherited declining congregations with few financial resources, no staff, and huge odds against them. Furthermore, neither pastor was full-time (at least, not on paper). What happened next was a work of the Holy Spirit bringing a white and African American church together. The two churches struck an agreement: Residence Park would use the facility in the later morning for a separate worship service. This went on for a few months, and after a time of "courtship," the pastors had an idea: Why not worship together? Of course, this made perfect sense to the two pastors, and both congregations were willing to try it because they saw they could be stronger together than they were apart. Today, the pastors take turns preaching every other Sunday, and at times they tag-team preach in order to build unity.

In 2007, Interbay Covenant Church in Seattle decided to close down and merge with another place of worship, Quest Church. Interbay was a sixty-five-year-old, traditional, urban, older, and mostly white church that had a vibrant youth ministry in the 1970s and '80s. However, the church of about seventy people started experiencing decline around 2000 as members began moving or passing away.[8]

On the other hand, Quest Church, founded in 2000, was a six-year-old, emerging, urban, multiethnic church plant that was growing by leaps and bounds. Quest was renting a warehouse from Interbay for its growing congregation and urban ministries, and a relationship was forged between the two pastors, Eugene Cho and Ray Bartel. Although it was a difficult decision for Interbay members to merge, they eventually decided to give Quest all their assets, including their church building and small warehouse. The congregation was kingdom-minded instead of tradition-minded, "giving themselves to the next generation."[9]

Another story of churches merging comes from Sioux Falls, South Dakota. Embrace United Methodist Church started in 2006 with forty people and is now averaging an estimated three thousand people across its three physical campuses and online community. Looking to expand to another campus in the Twin Cities, leadership approached another church to see if they wanted to merge into their church. The people of St. Croix Valley United Methodist Church were asked if they would give over their building, their identity, and their way of being so that Embrace could launch a new campus in their building. Three weeks after hearing the proposal, the members of St. Croix decided to merge with Embrace for the sake of making Christ known.[10]

Another positive example of churches merging occurred in Dayton, Ohio. Fort McKinley Church was a struggling, inner-city church with decreasing membership. No matter what the congregation tried, they could not get the church to grow. Losing hope, the forty-member congregation voted unanimously in 2008 to merge with another church while remaining at their current location. Merging with Ginghamsburg Church brought new life and hope to the faith community. Since the merger, attendance has increased from forty to more than four hundred, and there is a renewed focus on missional relationships with the surrounding neighborhood. The church is now considered one of Dayton's most vibrant, diverse, and exciting faith communities.[11]

The most segregated time in America is still Sunday mornings. While this is a reality in many places around the country, it is not a kingdom of God reality. Higher Ground, Residence Park, and the other faith communities mentioned here have broken barriers in a way that has resulted in a mosaic of believers; increased attendance and involvement; and created new opportunities to partner in outreach, children and youth ministry, and discipleship. What would it look like if more local churches broke down their walls and built bridges with one another?

Many congregations have become so isolated from one another that, even within their own faith tradition or denomination, people have virtually no connection to anybody else. Declining attendance overall leaves many local churches like Higher Ground and Residence Park with aging congregations and buildings that are difficult to maintain. The problems pile up, and it can be easy for pastors and churches to give up. What if leveraging resources and sharing burdens was more common among local churches? Yes, as you might expect, congregations can experience growing pains as they move from having their own space to sharing space to ultimately worshipping together in one service. It's not easy, but the results are worth the effort.

Many times the miracles God wants to provide are right in front of us, but we, as human beings, want to pick and choose how we want or expect God to work. In the society of Jesus's day, children were seen but not heard or acknowledged. They were on the low end of the social spectrum. By using a little boy's lunch to feed the masses, Jesus communicated that miracles can come through unexpected, seemingly insignificant, or mundane channels. In many cities and towns across the United States, there are local churches within the same faith tradition and denomination, separated only by a few miles and struggling to survive. Over the next decade, as churches face the possibility of closing their doors, the challenges of decline will create opportunities to turn desperation into innovation for churches that are willing to see beyond their own building, worship service, and traditions and to be in partnerships that make them better together than they would be on their own. What if the miracles for these local churches were already right in front of them? Churches would like to hit the jackpot of an inexplicable influx of new people from their community or a multimillion-dollar benefactor. By contrast, joining with another local church doesn't have the same appeal and requires us to suppress some of the less admirable aspects of our human nature. But what if doing so results in a stronger impact and witness for the combined community? Pastors and churches can't afford to be choosy about the miracles God wants to provide to us. Local churches and leaders can't afford to be picky and prideful during these times of spiritual starvation in our world. Partnership can create a witness similar to the first-century Christians who were leading others into the Christian faith by fulfilling Jesus's words to his disciples in John 13:35, "This is how everyone will know that you are my disciples, when you love each other."

73

The Point Church Shopping Strip

When Ginghamsburg Church announced plans to open a campus in Trotwood, Ohio, a suburb of Dayton, people did a double take. It's no secret that Dayton was hit hard by the 2008 recession, especially after the closure of the General Motors factory and the departure of National Cash Register. These and other closures took thousands of jobs out of the city. Dayton was even featured on *Forbes* magazine's list of the top ten fastest dying cities in America.

Fortunately, Dayton is slowly creeping back economically. But many areas of the city are still feeling the effects of decline. Trotwood was once a destination for people from surrounding parts of Ohio in the 1970s and '80s because it was thriving and even had the first mall in the area, the Salem Mall. Today, Walmart, Target, Applebee's, and numerous other businesses have closed in Trotwood. The vacant old restaurant buildings, empty commercial spaces, home foreclosures, and decreasing home values are what people notice at first glance.

Because of this, the perception is that Trotwood is an area of trouble and high crime. While Trotwood and surrounding areas have battled crime, the people of Trotwood are resilient and tight-knit. Nevertheless, Ginghamsburg Church didn't view expanding to Trotwood as a charity case, but rather as a way to live into their mission of transforming one life at a time while maintaining an investment in urban areas.

Fifteen years ago, the United Methodist Church's Miami Valley District purchased a shopping strip in Trotwood. A church was started in the shopping strip. Things went well until the pastor of the church experienced a moral failure. After that, the space sat empty. In fact, a young man was shot in the parking lot outside a bar in the shopping center.

When the district approached Ginghamsburg Church about the possibility of taking occupancy of the space in exchange for free rent and utilities for five years, Ginghamsburg Church saw this as an opportunity to use the space for God's glory, which is how Ginghamsburg's Point Campus came about. Ginghamsburg launched The Point Church on the Saturday of Easter weekend in 2012. The Point's focus was to build partnerships that would help revitalize the dying city. As a working-class city, every day seemed like the Bill Murray movie *Groundhog Day*. Any excitement usually revolved around high school football or bad press. The Point sought to serve the city in a way that would break the monotony and bring hope to the neighborhood.

The Point's partnership with the city of Trotwood has been a starting point for many outreach activities. For the last three years, The Point has partnered with the city to throw a block party. The first year, The Point took the lead and invited the city to come alongside. The city has begun to take the reins of this event for its people. Together The Point and the city of Trotwood have provided inflatables, children's games, fire trucks, the Trotwood Madison High School marching band, entertainment, food trucks, and fireworks. This is what The Point set out to do: to paint a picture of hope and possibility for the city of Trotwood. Sometimes it takes the church stepping up to encourage the city to build community from its citizenry.

The Point has also collaborated with the city to host an Easter egg hunt for the community. The Point stuffed thousands of eggs and scattered them in a field divided into sections for each age group. The Easter Bunny pays a visit and takes pictures with the kids, and there are special eggs with golden tickets that children can turn in for a gift.

Each fall as the weather turns cooler, The Point comes together for a monthly family movie night. The Point clears the worship center of all chairs. Families bring blankets. Some wear their pajamas. The Point provides the popcorn and a movie for families to enjoy. The church offers other sugary concessions for purchase. Families register for a door prize to be awarded at the end of the night.

As the tension between the public and police has grown recently across the country, The Point wanted to offer a platform for discussion and understanding. A young police officer in The Point's congregation was passionate about building a bridge between the public and the police. He organized, and The Point hosted, an evening of discussion called "Putting the Pieces Together." Police, community developers, and caring citizens from Trotwood, Dayton, and its suburbs, and even some from Cincinnati, had open and honest dialogue, and shared ideas about how The Point can change the relationship between the public and public servants. This was a popular event that quickly outgrew the capacity of The Point.

Following this event, The Point hosted another community engagement event called "Coffee with the Cops." Trotwood citizens were given the opportunity to get to know the local law enforcement officers who serve and protect their community. The church was a nonthreatening environment for this event centered on eliminating barriers that exist between law enforcement and citizens. Many great conversations took place, and people genuinely enjoyed each other's company. The police officers even bought the coffee and donuts!

These efforts culminated in a neighborhood kickball game with the kids from The Point and Fort McKinley Church and surrounding communities playing against Dayton police officers and the Harrison Township Fire Department. There were over fifty people on the field in a game that went well over an hour, along with a few hundred people sitting on the sidelines and enjoying pizza.

There are times we can catch glimpses of God. It doesn't happen too often on the news or the Internet, but it happened that night through a simple game of kickball and fellowship over pizza. There were no news crews out or media flooding the streets, but there was a spirit of reconciliation that is reminiscent of what Jesus encouraged.

None of these events cost The Point any money. As mentioned before, all the supplies were purchased by the police officers themselves. All The Point had to do was be open to sharing our space and volunteers to foster community. The police officers and firefighters desire to tear down barriers, and they are now in regular communication with the church about service opportunities and ways they can be involved with the general public. These relationships can happen in cities across America if local churches are willing to get out of their comfort zones and welcome in people who have similar values for the common good.

The Point has also partnered with the city's farmers' market to provide live music and sponsored a booth at the city's Harvest Walk each October. These are simple events that don't cost much and require few staff or servants, but which have the potential to reach the community and let them know about the church, its mission, and upcoming church events.

One of The Point's best partnerships has been with Trotwood Madison Schools. The schools have allowed us to distribute flyers

77

for The Point's events, which has been The Point's primary source of marketing. The Point designs, prints, and bundles flyers into stacks for each classroom. The only cost to us is the printing. In this way, The Point has built relationships that let us into the school to reach both teachers and students.

Ms. Tiffaney, The Point's children's ministry coordinator, has built bridges by reading to children at the Early Learning Center each week. The city had built new schools with government funds. However, there were only a handful of books, so the school didn't have a library or a librarian. Ms. Tiffaney spoke with the principal and organized a book drive. The Point put out word to all three campuses of Ginghamsburg Church. In a matter of weeks, The Point collected over ten thousand books! Servants from The Point and teachers came together to inspect and sort books using the school's system. The Point placed stickers inside each cover that said "Open a book and change your world. A gift from The Point Church." That year, a retired teacher volunteered as the school librarian. The book drive brought in books for all ages, so books for older kids were distributed at the upper elementary schools. There were duplicates of many books, so The Point was also able to send books home with children. The schoolchildren made thank-you cards to share with The Point's congregation. Today, the school operates with a full-time librarian and fully stocked library.

Trotwood is a community that loves local athletics, especially when it comes to football. The Point has capitalized on this as a way to reach the community. In 2014, the church provided dinner for the high school football team the night before the big game. The Point followed up at the game by passing out "Thunder-sticks" (noisemakers) emblazoned with the team logo to each fan as they entered the stadium. The following year, the girls' varsity soccer team came to church one Sunday and joined The Point's student ministry class. They came for prayer for a safe and injury-free season. At the end of the season, the church hosted a dinner for the team.

The Point has also celebrated hard-working teachers in the city by partnering with a local ice cream parlor to serve ice cream, complete with all the toppings, to teachers. The Point passed out large bags of chips to each teacher with stickers that said "You're all that and a bag of chips."

All these efforts may seem small in and of themselves, but taken together, The Point Church has built morale in a community that needs it, letting the community know that it is cared for and that the church will be there to help individuals and communities grow stronger together.

The Point's Business Partners

The Point loves partnering with local businesses. In the same shopping plaza where the church is located, there is a pizza shop owned by Turkish immigrants. When the church started, it worshipped on Saturday nights. After worship, The Point opened up its café, and people could purchase a few slices of the shop's pizza and a drink for two dollars. The Point bought two party pizzas every Saturday for two years. The Point has continued to do business with the pizza place for children's and teen events. During the block party, the church orders fifty party pizzas. The Point staff has enjoyed countless meals there. Through the many brief interactions with the pizza shop, the church has formed relationships with the owner and his family. When other church staff members pick up their orders, the pizza workers ask them where the "priest" is. They have asked members about social issues, money, and membership in The Point's congregation. The

Point has piqued their interest, just by doing business with them regularly. The owners and the staff of the pizza shop may never attend The Point's church services, but the church has been able to help them out simply by the proximity and continued patronage, and, hopefully, it's modeling the love of Christ through the many interactions.

The Ice Cream Parlour has also been an excellent connection for The Point. The owner has served up countless scoops of ice cream at ice cream socials and at the teacher appreciation event at The Point. During a chilly, outdoor movie night, she traded in ice cream cones for cups of hot cocoa. The owner brings her own setup and serves the ice cream and cocoa herself, freeing up The Point's staff to make connections with the community.

The Point's Building Partners

The Point shares space with a YMCA and The Point–Fort Food Pantry. While sharing space has its challenges, the benefits are greater. Members of The Point promote each other's ministries and events. We serve clients in the food pantry. The food pantry serves the community around us. Servants from the church and staff from the YMCA work together to keep the flowerbeds in and around the parking lot clean and free of weeds and trash. Because The Point shares space with these other organizations and ministries, people come who may otherwise never darken the doors of a church.

To keep the challenges of sharing space to a minimum, each month The Point holds a partners' meeting. This is a time to discuss challenges and find solutions, share information about upcoming events, ensure that shared spaces are available for those events, and address cleaning issues, pest control, and building maintenance needs.

Clubhouse

Clubhouse is a free, faith-based after-school and summer program for elementary-aged children with limited opportunities. Clubhouse trains and mentors teens to become leaders in the seven Clubhouse locations in Dayton and other Miami Valley neighborhoods.

During the school year, each day of the week has a designated focus. On "faith day," children are led by teens in interactive games, crafts, and discussions about faith. On "education day," kids can get help with homework and reading and do fun experiments. Clubhouse also focuses on sports, art, and recreation. Teens design activities individually or with co-leaders and teach them to the children. During the summer, teen interns plan field trips, activities, community service projects, and educational activities for children. Teens learn to lead, and children who are typically underserved form relationships, receive tutoring, and have the opportunity for recreation and day camps.

New Path

New Path is the outreach arm of Ginghamsburg UMC. It offers many services to the community, such as a food pantry, a furniture ministry, a car ministry, a dental ministry, a medical equipment ministry, and more. New Path also has a few retail locations that solicit and resell donated items in good condition. The income from these stores goes back to New Path to support its many ministries. In Trotwood, there are two New Path ministries, both located in the same shopping strip as The Point. The food pantry helps feed the Trotwood community with donations from church members and food from the food bank. Isaiah's Threads sells gently used clothing at low prices as well as fair-trade merchandise. Clients of the food pantry can qualify for clothing vouchers that allow them to purchase a number of items for one dollar each.

New Path also has created a time bank, which is a return to bartering. The time bank allows people who typically find themselves in a line, having to qualify for assistance, to trade goods or services with another member of the time bank. This is an excellent way to offer assistance while helping those with less to recognize that they do have something to offer. In this way, it can help to even the playing field between the lower and middle classes. This is a model that requires very little overhead expense to meet a wide range of needs. Each person who signs up to be part of the time bank lists the kinds of goods or services they have to offer. Anytime a person contributes time or talent to someone else in the program, they earn hours that can be spent to buy something else. Some examples of items traded through the time bank are fresh-baked bread or cakes, help creating a budget, haircuts, car repairs, photography sessions, and gardening services.

In 2015, The Point became the property manager of the shopping strip. The Point is renovating and cleaning up empty storefronts and seeking to rent them to businesses that will benefit the city of Trotwood and meet the needs of its citizens.

Other Examples Throughout the Country

Northwest Children's Outreach is a faith-based, nonprofit organization dedicated to helping families in the Portland, Oregon, area. Operating out of several churches (Westside Church of Christ, Rolling Hills Community Church, and The Chapel) in different communities, the Northwest Children's Outreach fills the needs of families by providing clothing, infant care products, diapers, formula, and many other essentials. They collect resources for children and distribute the goods to local care providers who meet directly with and prescreen the children.[12]

After the city of Detroit, Michigan, filed for bankruptcy in 2013, its citizens faced enormous needs. Nonprofits, churches, foundations, and entrepreneurs stepped up to meet citizens' needs in areas where city services are insufficient or nonexistent. For example, Chris Lambert, pastor of Ekklesia Church, launched a service called Life Remodeled. Using an estimated five thousand volunteers and donated supplies, Life Remodeled provides low-income families with new houses, along with budgeting, financial lessons, and support to help them keep their new homes. According to the *Detroit Free Press*, the group "plans to board up vacant homes, renovate some homes, and build one new home from scratch, all part of the largest volunteer revitalization effort in recent Detroit history."[13]

In Charleston, South Carolina, Mount Pleasant Presbyterian Church and the Greater Goodwill AME Church decided to team up with the Charleston County School District to help the district's lowest performing readers close the achievement gap. The resulting nonprofit is now known as I-Beam and operates a lunchtime literacy and mentoring program that connects volunteer mentors with students in grades two through five who scored below the 25th percentile on MAP testing, who qualify for free or reduced lunch, or who are recommended into the program by their teacher. Each week during the school year, an adult mentors a student at his or her school for one hour, eating lunch and reading one-to-one with the student. Since its founding in 2011, I-Beam has grown from fifty-five volunteers from two churches, working with one school and two grade levels, to more than two hundred and fifty volunteers from sixteen organizations and churches, impacting students in six elementary schools.[14]

Since 2008, funds have been cut in more than 80 percent of US school districts. Disciplines such as music, art, and foreign language are often the first programs to go.[15] New Hope Presbyterian Church is just one of many nonprofits that has helped keep music alive in schools in Orange County, California. Seven years ago, the New Hope congregation discovered that the nearby Willard Intermediate School did not have a music instructor and could not afford to give the students a regular music program. The church decided to do something. Today, the church has a music academy that operates out of its building and hosts a four-day camp where, for ten dollars each, these young students work with Stevie Wonder's percussionist, Munyungo Jackson. Today, the four-day camp is merely a precursor to more rehearsals that culminate in an already legendary November concert called "Hope Alive," a fund-raiser for other school music programs.[16]

One of the best examples of how a 501(c)(3) can help churches is the Dream Center in Los Angeles. In 1994, Matthew Barnett began pastoring a small church in Los Angeles. Times were tough for the church with little activity and decreasing attendance. The church's young pastor decided to set up his office outside on the sidewalk, asking people who passed by how he could help them. Eventually, this outreach grew, and the church came back to life. Barnett noticed the old, vacant Queen of Angels Hospital in Echo Park and imagined a place where God's love could be offered to the homeless, the addicted, the victims of sex trafficking and domestic violence, the foster youth, and anyone who needed food and hope.[17] Thus began the Dream Center, a volunteer-driven organization that finds and fills the needs of more than eighty thousand individuals and families each month through mobile hunger relief and medical programs, residential rehabilitation programs, a shelter for victims of human trafficking, transitional housing for homeless families, foster care intervention programs, job and life skills training, counseling, basic education, Bible studies, and more.

Other churches choose to serve as a bridge between existing nonprofits, schools, and businesses in their communities. One example of this type of partnership is The Well at Springfield, a four-year-old missional church plant in Jacksonville, Florida. "We want to be a connector between different people that otherwise wouldn't meet," pastor Susan Rogers said. "And we want to connect with what God is already doing through multiple agents."[18] An example she cited is The Well's Laundromat of Love ministry. Held twice a year, it features members of the Cooperative Baptist congregation paying for the washing and drying of clothes for a two-hour period on a Sunday morning.

Partnerships are crucial for ministry now more than ever. Partnering is also the biblical model for ministry. In the story of Jesus feeding the multitudes, why did Jesus gather people into groups of fifty and one hundred? Jesus wanted order and structure to facilitate the miracle he was about to do. Jesus wanted the disciples to *distribute*. In the midst of the miracles, order, system, and structure were taking place through partnership. The groups of fifty and one hundred had to patiently wait their turn and work with each disciple giving out food. The partnership created over those few hours was dependent on trust rather than pride.

Sometimes God calls a church to create a new ministry or to support a church member in the creation of a new ministry. Other times a church needs to look to the organizations already in place, to the people who already know their communities and serve them well, for ways that they can purposefully further God's mission through those existing organizations. Even when churches are called to begin something new, they will not succeed in fulfilling their visions from God by working in isolation. In order to bring about the kind of miraculous multiplication of efforts God has in mind for our communities, churches must pursue every strategically appropriate opportunity for synergy they can.

Chapter 5

FUND-RAISING AND GRANTS FOR PROJECTS

Never think you need to apologize for asking someone to give to a worthy objective, any more than as though you were giving him an opportunity to participate in high-grade investment. The duty of giving is as much his as the duty of asking yours. Whether or not he should give to that particular enterprise, and if so, how much, it is for him alone to decide.

—John D. Rockefeller

He replied, "You give them something to eat." But they said, "We have no more than five loaves of bread and two fish—unless we go and buy food for all these people." (Luke 9:13)

As revenue decreases with the decline of the generation of faithful givers, churches are tightening budgets, reducing staff sizes, and canceling outreach to surrounding communities. The Christian market research firm the Barna Group reports an overall decrease in giving in nearly every study they have conducted since the year 2000. Also, Barna notes that only "12% of born again Christians tithe."[1] The financial future of the church looks bleak.

87

However, things are not always as they appear. Although giving to churches has steadily decreased throughout the years, giving has actually increased within the broader culture. Indiana State University's Lilly Family School of Philanthropy released a study showing two longstanding trends in giving: first, people are giving more, and to more organizations per year than ever before; secondly, of the seventeen categories of recipients that the study tracked, only donations to religious organizations and foundations have been down year after year.[2]

Why is giving in general on the rise, yet declining for churches? The explanation lies in large part in institutional distrust and disillusionment. People no longer unreservedly trust the church. The church's traditional practice of asking its congregants to donate to a general fund that is divided up to pay staff salaries, maintain facilities, and fund community outreach is no longer palatable in today's culture. This old, single-budget model is based on a level of trust that, for better or worse, no longer exists. The church must adapt to the current culture and implement new models of fund-raising.

This lack of trust stems, at least in part, from the exponential increase in the availability of information, and a resulting expectation for increased transparency in decision making. As a pastor, this can actually be seen as an opportunity to share the responsibilities of strategizing, raising funds, and budgeting with the congregation. There are a few things a pastor needs to keep in mind while brainstorming new models of fund-raising. Potential givers want to know:

- Does my giving make a difference?

- Do I matter to my faith community?

- How will my resources be used?

- What is the vision I'm giving toward, and what is the plan for reaching it?

- How can I get involved in the ministry I am supporting financially?

Put simply, people want to know how and where their money is spent, how successfully an organization fulfills its stated mission, and whether or not they will have a say in the vision beyond that first decision to write a check or not. The younger generations of givers support missions, not institutions. This means that everything a pastor communicates about giving should stress ministry, not upkeep.[3]

A pastor needs to make sure the congregation knows and has bought into a given vision, and when it has, this vision should drive the investment of its resources. Not only should pastors talk about the church's visions, but they must also speak about the step-by-step plan for moving toward the visions. Another way to encourage people to give is to find ways they can physically get involved in the ministries they are supporting financially. Some folks prefer to give to ministries in which they have an active role. Likewise, donors want to know if others have experienced life change because of their generosity. This means that hearing or seeing personal stories of change can have a powerful effect.

Today, one of the most important factors for giving is a church's financial transparency. Pastors often hesitate to give constant updates on projects, especially when the expectations aren't being met. Yet, providing honest updates on the progress made because of financial contributions breeds trust with the congregation.

Some Examples

Special Mission Projects

In 2004, senior pastor Mike Slaughter of Ginghamsburg UMC felt that his congregation was being called by the Holy Spirit to address the humanitarian crisis in Darfur, Sudan, a crisis that has been identified by the United Nations as one of the worst in the world. During the Advent season of 2004, the pastor challenged his church to spend only one-half on Christmas gifts of what they would normally spend and donate the remainder to what was called the Sudan Project in a "Miracle Offering."

The church responded in a huge way and has continued giving to the Sudan Project ever since. Since early 2005, the church (in partnership with the United Methodist Committee on Relief) has funded three primary projects in the region: a sustainable agriculture program impacting up to 85,000 people, a sanitation project including nineteen water yards and almost fifteen hundred latrines, and nearly two hundred and fifty schools serving close to thirty thousand students.[4]

Rev. Slaughter cast the vision for reaching Sudan, and the church bought into it. Not only was the need addressed; a plan to accomplish the vision was developed. The congregation is updated regularly on the Sudan Project by seeing the actual numbers and other facts about the projects in progress. Along with the annual Christmas offering, people can visit a website about the project and donate toward it online. The numbers and lives impacted from this project speak for themselves. By 2014, a total of nearly seven million dollars had been invested by Ginghamsburg and its partner churches, schools, and businesses.

Recently, the church pledged to raise one million dollars over five years toward ending preventable deaths from malaria. Partnering with Imagine No Malaria, a ministry of The United Methodist Church, Ginghamsburg seeks to eradicate malaria deaths in Sudan. Since 2013, thirty thousand mosquito nets have been purchased and education on their use given to the women and children in one of South Sudan's most vulnerable sites.[5]

Many of the projects churches undertake are prime fundraising opportunities. Finding people who have a passion for particular projects or programs can expand access to funds even beyond the walls of the church. This is where partnerships and being involved in the community come in handy.

Grants

Grants are often a mystery to pastors and are overlooked as a potential funding source for new projects or programs that line up with vision and mission. Many communities have affordable grant-writing classes available, so one idea is to designate a pastor or church member to take those classes and then work to write grants and train others in grant-writing as well. A few pastors and other church leaders took local grant-writing classes, then used their new skills to search out funding streams for various ministries of the church, from our work with children to meeting the physical needs of others in our community.

Embrace is fortunate to have received significant funds from these sources. After conducting a thorough feasibility study about North Limestone neighborhood storm-water improvement, Eco-Gro, an environmental water engineering company, reached out to Embrace as a strong candidate for grant funds due to its key location and need for storm-water improvements.

The total grant amount Embrace received was $215,745. The funded improvements included retrofitting an existing detention area, installation of drainage inlets and a storm sewer to collect runoff, removal of 2,300 square feet of asphalt parking, retrofitting 11,000 square feet of existing asphalt with grass pavers to reduce runoff to the adjacent property, removal of approximately 2,250 square feet of impervious pavement in the back parking lot, and replacement with a bio-retention facility and curb to treat runoff and reduce runoff to the adjacent property. These modifications would significantly improve the state of storm-water runoff for the church and a number of neighbors by reducing flooding and standing water issues.

Embrace Church takes advantage of free programing facilitated by the state of Kentucky to provide nutritious meals for kids during the school year and summer. The Kids Café Program provides free meals and snacks to low-income families. These meals are cooked at the church. In addition to providing meals to hungry kids, Kids Café programs also offer a safe place, where under the supervision of trustworthy staff, a child can get involved in educational, recreational, and social activities that draw on existing community programs and often include family members. During the school year, Embrace provides dinner four times a week to children. Despite federally funded programs, too many hungry children are falling through the cracks, especially during the evening hours. Kids Café provides children with more than just food; it also offers them emotional nourishment critical to healthy development, improving their self-image, and enhancing their ability to learn.

Because of Embrace's role as a Kid's Café location, an organization called God's Pantry recommended Embrace Church for an Arby's food giveaway in 2013. This giveaway was part of a community engagement project where Arby's sets up their truck at designated locations, serves free food to children and families in the community, and organizes a time of family fun. Along with being selected as a location, Embrace received a $2,500 grant that was used for children's ministry at the church.

One caution is worth noting here: if your congregation is going to use grant money, you need to be aware of the specific demands of the granting organization. If their expectations of the work conflict with your mission and vision, you might want to look elsewhere for funding. Let the ministry drive the funding choices, not the other way around.

Crowdfunding

Another skill that will prove particularly helpful in the coming years is the ability to raise money through the use of crowdfunding sources. Crowdfunding websites are becoming an increasingly popular tool to help churches raise money for specific ministries. Again, at Embrace, crowdfunding sites have raised money for ministries, from making laundry detergent for our impoverished neighbors to providing diapers for families in the community. These sites are not difficult to use, but it is beneficial to have a person who can correctly set up your effort's page and ensure that it gets the sort of attention necessary to make it successful. There are literally billions of dollars being raised on crowdfunding sites around the world; there is no reason for the church to stand on the sidelines.[6]

People may be reluctant to try new ways of producing revenue for the church, but Proverbs 13:22 tells us the wealth of sinners is stored up for the righteous. In this case, the church ought to be willing to consider a variety of funding sources for the good work of the Lord. It may be good to start with a relatively small project and seek out a grant from your denomination or another trusted Christian organization as a way to help church members begin to trust in grant-writing as a way to pay for ministries of the church. Start slowly with crowdfunding by asking for a small amount of money for a specific need. When church members see that it works, they will be more open to the idea of utilizing these tools again in the future.

The 501(c)(3)

Churches have tough jobs. They must spread the good news of Jesus Christ, and, as an integral component of doing so, they must also strive to meet the tangible needs of their surrounding communities. Homelessness, hunger, illiteracy, and addictions present challenges to pastors who already struggle to maintain their buildings and pay the bills with the available financial resources. Frustration and hopelessness can begin to overwhelm the pastor.

A partnership that can greatly assist a church is a 501(c)(3), a nonprofit organization that has been approved by the Internal Revenue Service as a tax-exempt, charitable organization. These organizations continually seek grants and fund-raise to combat the ills and meet the needs of society. They already have the structures in place and the relationships in the neighborhood to effectively help people. It is often easier to get grant money through a nonprofit than through a church. Why not partner with them?

Back at Ginghamsburg UMC, north of Dayton, Ohio, three 501(c)(3) nonprofit organizations were founded by church members to help the church carry out its missions. In 2001, New Path became the umbrella agency for outreach ministries at Ginghamsburg and currently operates seventeen separate community service ministries within the Dayton area, including two food pantries as well as car, furniture, clothing, medical equipment, pet care, rent/ utility assistance, and other ministries.

Ginghamsburg and New Path recently partnered with other organizations in the Fort McKinley neighborhood that want to revitalize the historic 1930s Dayton neighborhood and help more families attain home ownership through a project called Fort McKinley Homes. This project aims to build new, single-family, affordable Energy Star homes with a lease-to-purchase arrangement. Families selected for the Fort McKinley Homes Project pay rent arranged to be affordable to households earning 50 percent of the area median income or below, starting out at less than six hundred dollars per month. After renting the home for fifteen years, the families will then have the option to purchase the home at a reduced acquisition price determined by HomeStart.

According to Greg Smith, a developer with Oberer Land Developers, the partnership with Ginghamsburg and New Path proved to be the key in this project moving forward. He stated,

> There is fierce competition for stimulus dollars, and our group had already applied and been denied twice for federal grant funding. It was only when we partnered with the Fort McKinley Campus of Ginghamsburg Church and The New Path, Inc., that we were awarded the Neighborhood Stabilization Funds. Ginghamsburg brought a connection with the neighborhood and its residents while New Path brought a holistic approach to urban renewal. Combining the high quality of these homes with the support and stability factors made a strong case for the Fort McKinley Homes Program.[7]

A frightening question every church, both parishioner and pastor, must ask is, "If this church were to close its doors tomorrow, would anybody care or even notice?" Fort McKinley asked this same question when they merged with Ginghamsburg Church in 2008. As a result of their efforts, they have seen the neighborhood crime rate drop significantly since Ginghamsburg Church started a community development initiative in partnership with The New Path, Harrison Township, and Oberer Companies. In 2012, Harrison Township reported 198 crime-related incidents. In 2013, that number decreased by 13 percent to 172. As of July 31, 2014, crime had dropped significantly to eighty-nine incidents, resulting in a 55 percent decrease from 2012.[8]

Grants and fund-raising initiatives do not fall upon organizations like money magically falling from the sky. They must be sought after with intentionality and effort. As with the disciples and the hungry crowd, the easy solution for us today would be to acknowledge the needs and then turn the people away. Instead, Jesus's disciple Andrew dared to see the makings of a miracle that no one else recognized, and it happened to be directly in front of him. The successful stories of grants and fund-raisers highlighted above didn't happen because these local churches were special. What makes them unique is their ability to seek out something that's available to all.

Chapter 6

OUTREACH ON A BUDGET

If your church claims evangelism is a priority, you have to be able to back up that claim with dollars allocated in your budget. Otherwise you're just blowing smoke.

—*Rick Warren*

> When they had plenty to eat, he said to his disciples, "Gather up the leftover pieces, so that nothing will be wasted." (John 6:12)

Many churches cut outreach when money gets tight, prioritizing building maintenance and their Sunday worship celebration instead. If the vision and mission of the church involves reaching the lost, outreach is essential. This chapter explores ways to cut the cost of outreach without cutting outreach.

Too often, pastors and churches think that they must have huge budgets to reach their communities. This idea is not true. In fact, some of the best ministry can happen when churches are forced to be creative with the resources available to them. Questions to prompt this creative thinking include:

1. Are there members within the church who are willing to donate their time and expertise (e.g., in tutoring, performing car maintenance, cooking)?

2. Are there congregants who live in the neighborhood and are willing to host dinners?

3. Are there members who are willing to move into the community in order to become "missionaries" in the neighborhood?

4. What are the places in the community that need volunteers?

Outreach can mean a variety of things in different communities depending on the context, culture, and setting. What works in an urban area may not work in a rural or suburban community. Before churches choose to prioritize outreach, it's crucial for them to understand both the felt needs as well as the community's assets. All communities have both; some just require a bit more digging to uncover. If a person is new to an area, there is nobody better to talk with than city officials who have a read on the community. One of the most informative things a pastor can do is ride along with a police officer on duty for traffic stops. All citizens can do this simply by contacting their police department. One pastor did this while he was still new at his church, and here's what he said about the experience:

> Not too long ago, I took four hours to do something that I've never tried before: I decided to ride with the [police department]. After setting up the ride, I showed up at my selected time and began the process of being acclimated to the new environment.
>
> From the attention to detail, to the checklists, to the meticulous care he took with his stuff, I knew Officer Michaels [name has been changed] was experienced. When I found out that he was a twenty-five-year veteran of the force, I was surprised because he looked young. He told me that the one thing [his department] isn't short of is experience. These are officers who care deeply for their job and, as a result, have been around for a long time. It was obvious to me that this wasn't just a job; it was a calling to serve.

When we rode around the city, I learned about how new areas have been annexed over the years, how the traffic has escalated, and how people seem to get angry more quickly than ever before. When I asked Officer Michaels what the hardest part of his job was, he said it was heroin. He estimated that 50 percent of his work was drug-related or theft that was drug-related. [The drug epidemic of the broader region also enveloped his town].

Sometimes it may feel like our community is exempt from these problems, but the truth is that we are as vulnerable as anyone.

I ended our time together asking him, what could our church do for the community and what could we do for the people [in his town]?

His response was simple, profound, and biblical (although I suspect he didn't know it at the time). He looked me in the eyes and said, "We need the church to be a resource. As officers we know how to stop the crime, but we don't always know how to get the people the help they need."[1]

Imagine that: a church that is called to help the people. That's something I think we can all get behind.

Going on a police ride-along and talking to public officials and longtime residents can give a local church insight into what outreach should look like in a given area. And it's free! Demographic studies can be a start, but "feet on the street" can connect names with faces, problems with specific areas, and resources with the people who need them.

Community Prayer Box and Chalkboard

One of the first things The Point did was to create a prayer request station outside the church building. Servants built it from pallets and donated materials. The Point keeps prayer request cards and a basket of golf pencils available. People can fill out their request card and drop it in a secured mailbox. These requests are collected once or twice each week, compiled, and sent to The

Point's staff and care pastor network. It's simple, but the prayer box has made it easy for food pantry clients, YMCA members, patrons of the pizza shop and BMV, and other passersby to request prayer.

Another simple project made of donated materials and built by servants is a giant chalkboard that sits outside The Point's building year-round. The Point writes prompts, such as: "My favorite part of summer is…"; "My mom taught me…"; "I am grateful for…"; and "My favorite teacher…" It is a fun way for the community to interact with the church.

There are ways to reach out without breaking the budget that can serve as entry points to let unchurched men, women, and children in your community know about your weekly worship services and other programs. Once again, partnering with other area churches in these endeavors allows a greater impact as finances, volunteers, and other resources can be shared. For example, five churches in Cedar Rapids, Iowa, unite each year for their Convoy of Hope to share the good news of Christ and to bring groceries to families in the neighborhood who are in need of help. While an estimated seven hundred volunteers gather on the grounds of a local middle school to distribute twenty-five thousand pounds of food, the event also provides medical and dental screenings, balloons, haircuts, a job fair, live music, and theater.[2]

One Donut at a Time

One of the things Embrace Church has become known for in the city of Lexington is truly embodying their name. Without a doubt, Embrace Church is one of the most diverse congregations in the entire state of Kentucky. Part of the "embrace" that people feel is hospitality. While meeting for worship in the Kentucky Theatre, Embrace set up its hospitality table outside for anybody who wanted coffee and donuts. It didn't matter if they came inside for worship or not. As a church, Embrace tries to communicate that anybody is welcome no matter what. A hospitality team and table are another small but mighty element in reaching the community; it makes people feel welcome, especially when they can bring their coffee and donut into worship with them. Many churches don't have greeters at the doors or any type of hospitality in place because they may not expect anybody new to come to their church. When churches are struggling, the first things they cut are sometimes the most important.

Unfortunately, our welcome donuts were prohibitively expensive. Embrace didn't want to give up that part of the church's identity just because they couldn't fund it. It was time to investigate other options to cut expenses while still welcoming visitors and members in a tangible way. This led to a local donut shop called North Limestone Coffee & Donuts becoming a community partner.

North Lime, as this generous business is affectionately called, was a start-up shop at the time and still partners regularly with local nonprofits and churches, giving back to the community while providing great service. The donut flavors were wild and eccentric—Guinness beer–battered donuts, toppings like fried chicken and bacon, and Easter donuts with Peeps on them. Embrace worked out a deal with the shop to purchase a few dozen fresh donuts, while the shop would give us any leftover donuts they had for free. This saved the church hundreds of dollars every month and built a lasting partnership with a new business while providing outreach offerings to the community. Embrace went from having generic glazed donuts to having the best donuts in Lexington—for a fraction of the cost. A small gesture like this went a long way to improve hospitality while operating on a shoestring budget.

Just like the little boy's five loaves and two fish, it sometimes seemed Embrace had leftover donuts for days. Everything needed was provided, and it came from outside the offering plate.

Photography

Another way Embrace Church was able to give back to the arts was by allowing one of their members, freelance photographer Matt Baker, to have a studio in a room that was underutilized. Baker was allowed to store equipment and use the classroom as a photo studio, and, in exchange, he would provide his services to Embrace free of charge. Baker started by taking photos of children with the Easter Bunny at our community egg hunt. At Christmastime he provided photo packages for parishioners, which also turned into a popular church fund-raiser. Baker would take pictures of many of Embrace's homeless parishioners. For some of the folks, it was the first nice picture that someone had taken of them in a long time. Baker also took Christmas photos in exchange for thermal socks that were then distributed to Embrace's friends in need. Embrace was able to distribute a few thousand pairs of socks during the winter months as a result of this outreach idea. This didn't cost the church anything. Baker also donated the use of his photo-quality printer and his time. Plus, there weren't layers of approval processes because Embrace was in the habit of encouraging this type of creativity from its laypeople.

Laundry Detergent

As Embrace Church found itself reaching out to all people, especially folks in lower-income situations, a need that became apparent—one that many people take for granted—is clean clothes. The church had a clothing bank that made sure people had clothes. However, once people have the clothes, how do you help them keep those clothes clean? In shelters, the environment can be rough. It's impossible to carry all of one's belongings, let alone keep those belongings clean. This launched a micro-business endeavor by Embrace's outreach pastor, Justin Barringer. Embrace was able to provide hundreds of loads of bio-degradable, hypoallergenic, low-suds laundry detergent to members and guests of Embrace. This outreach effort raised nearly four hundred dollars to buy supplies through an online fund-raising campaign and sales from initial batches. The next step was to go bigger. Barringer wanted to teach the skills of making detergent to anybody who wanted to learn. A few Saturday mornings of making detergent brought together folks from all walks of life. The stated reason for gathering was to make detergent, but something even greater happened: relationships were formed. After the Monday night service called the Gathering, which included not only a worship service and meal but also take-home food baskets for anybody in need, each person had the opportunity to buy a canister of detergent for only fifty cents. Each canister could wash over thirty loads of laundry! The money that was generated from the project went right back into the laundry detergent ministry. Additionally, because people were learning skills, they were able to give back through their talents as well. The outreach only cost Embrace the initial startup money. After that, the project was self-sustaining. Embrace's lack of resources created an entrepreneurial spirit and allowed church members to tap into the passions and gifts of people right in front of them.

Too often churches let the needs in their communities over-whelm them. The mind-set is if they can't do it all, then they can't do anything. The disciples must have felt similarly, especially when they saw some fifteen to twenty thousand people starving for lunch. God often takes our "not enough" and transforms it into something miraculous.

God's Pantry

Another gap identified in the area of nutrition is that many of the elementary school students come back to school in the fall underweight, and not because they were playing all summer long. Many children face hunger during the summer when school is not in session. Kids Café provides lunches and dinner all summer long. Through all of Embrace Church's food programs, the church became known in the community as a place where people could get a warm meal. The best part of this outreach was that it didn't cost the church a dime. The truth is that many of these programs already exist and are federally funded, with churches sought as preferred partners. Embrace didn't need to re-create the wheel or make the excuse of not having enough money to feed people. It merely had to offer itself as a conduit for what was already available. There are plenty of nonprofits and government programs willing to pay for services if the church will let them.

Local versus Global Missions

As a new faith community in the inner city, Embrace Church had to have an outward focus to be a light in the community. That outreach happened primarily through meals, a food and clothing bank, and a community garden. In year one, the church's annual budget was under one hundred thousand dollars, made possible in part by renting space in the historic downtown Kentucky Theatre for $130 a week. Embrace had great unpaid servants, including musicians, who would arrive early every Sunday morning to set up for a worshipful atmosphere. Embrace Church became known as a church with a little budget but a huge heart for the city of Lexington. With such a lean budget, Embrace wanted to strategically invest in what matched the values of the church. It is often said that a person's priorities can be clearly ascertained by looking at his or her calendar and checkbook. The same can be said about a local church. How do they spend their resources of time and money? Because Embrace focused so much on the city of Lexington, the one area of missions and outreach Embrace neglected for the first few years was overseas mission trips. The church supported some missionaries who were sent out from the church, but Embrace had not organized any teams to travel together to other countries.

All that changed when one of Embrace's parishioners had an overseas mission experience, then developed an even deeper connection with the country of Ethiopia when they adopted an Ethiopian child. As an outgrowth, Embrace began promoting an upcoming mission trip to Ethiopia, yet we had no idea what to expect or even how to go about sending out missionaries. Somehow, we managed to sign up ten brave souls, including my wife and me. Embrace raised thirty thousand dollars for travel and ministry projects between church fund-raisers, personal funds, and private donations. Many had never been on an overseas mission trip and experienced culture shock due to both language barriers and the extreme poverty of the mission location. In Ethiopia, the team worked long, hard days repairing huts. We also participated in mercy ministries with local churches that were already doing outreach, and provided ongoing sponsorships for some of the children whom team members encountered through a Christian nonprofit public charity called Transformation Love. Five years later, team members still receive cards, handwritten letters, and school pictures from the children they support. It is a connection that will not be taken for granted.

Two years later, another team from Embrace Church went to Ethiopia because of the relationships that had been established there. The second trip bore more fruit, as that group was better able to focus on the team's strengths and the ministries where they felt called to serve. Between the two trips, over sixty thousand dollars had been invested.

While a short-term mission trip is a great experience for any Christian at some point, the heartbreaking thing was to consider the greater impact sixty thousand dollars might have made had it been invested instead in local Ethiopian leaders who would multiply their work without the travel expenses, without the lost time and money training new workers, and with the many added benefits of actually working in their own community.[3]

Congregations must consider Jesus's directive in Matthew 25:40, "I assure you that when you have done it for one of the least of these brothers and sisters of mine, you have done it for me." In doing so, a church should attempt to discern whether its members are called specifically to travel to a particular mission field, or whether they might better enable a group of people to break cycles of poverty and injustice by teaching job skills where they are, helping to start co-ops where they are, and participating in microfinancing to help start local businesses. And when people *are* called to travel to a mission site, perhaps it is these same ministries that will do the most good where they travel: empowering the local people in whatever ways the local people have decided they need empowerment. The prayer is that ministry will be multiplied beyond a single trip, and that a group of missionaries will serve where they can make the most impact.

Jesus took people beyond receiving miracles to taking part in the miracles. The example seen in the Gospels is Jesus's interactions with the disciples. At the beginning, the disciples merely watched him in action and then asked Jesus questions afterward. That changed in the feeding of the multitudes when the disciples began participating *with* Jesus in the miracle. They helped identify the resources at hand of loaves and fish, and then those were multiplied right before their eyes. They were blessed as they distributed the food and awed as they collected the leftovers. Without God, there would have been no miracle, but they were clearly on mission together as a team. Later in the Gospels, Jesus would send the disciples out two by two to minister in every surrounding city. When they returned, the disciples reported to Jesus all the miracles that had taken place. Ministry was now coming *from* the disciples. It did not happen overnight. It was a slow progression, but they were living into the power they were receiving from Jesus. The Apostle Paul later hits on God's aim in equipping the local church and its leaders by saying in Ephesians 4:12, "[God's] purpose was to equip God's people for the work of serving and building up the body of Christ." The work of ministry should progress from ministering *to* individuals, to ministering *with* individuals, and eventually seeing ministry *from* individuals.

After coming to this realization, Embrace adapted their missions philosophy. The pastor came back fired up from Ethiopia. He had discovered he was not cut out for overseas missions, but his trip did reinforce in him his call to reach his neighbors individually and as a church. As he began to pray about what Embrace's outreach would be to its neighbors and the nations, the pastor wanted to empower and equip people for the work of ministry and freedom in their own lives. As Embrace Church's ministry morphed into a multisite strategy, the church leaders discovered a Latino population living in the trailer park behind the church. Nearby, there was a growing refugee community from the Congo, Burundi, Ghana, and other African countries. The United States is in the midst of another "Golden Age" of immigration, and God is bringing the nations to the communities surrounding many churches.

As relationships were built with these new friends, it was an opportunity to train leaders. Embrace began a Spanish-language Bible study and a worship service led by folks from that community. Then, the vision spread to the refugee community; within a couple of months, a Burundian church plant began to use the facility to hold a worship service. All three congregations participated in one another's services and enjoyed fellowship dinners together. In a way, Embrace found it was participating in overseas missions without leaving home, without the exorbitant costs, and with much greater efficacy.

Consider the story of 12th Street, where a group of people became true missionaries to their local community. The Rock/ La Roca (a church that would eventually merge with Embrace) had to find creative ways to reach the surrounding neighborhood. Perhaps its best-known example is what is known as 12th Street. In 2003, several attendees from The Rock/La Roca moved onto 12th Street near the church. In total, four houses were occupied by church members from all different walks of life. Seminary students, recent college graduates, a teacher, a rescue mission cook, a social worker, and a nurse moved into the community with the sole purpose of befriending the neighbors and providing hospitality and friendship to them. Communal meals were shared at least four times per week, followed by a time of worship and prayer at least once during those times. One of the 12th Street participants said, "During prayer one Monday evening, I opened my eyes and glanced around the candlelit living room, and it dawned on me that this is the kingdom of God. In that room, people of different races, socioeconomic realities, sexual orientations, and life situations were joined together in pouring out our hearts to God. I felt God's love for each of us that night in a tangible way. It was a holy moment."

The Point Church in Trotwood has found itself in a situation similar to that of Embrace Church: being called to global missions without leaving home. As the campus pastor of The Point Church, I can rarely be found in my office. I station myself in a portion of the building that has become a café space. Since the church shares the building with the YMCA and a local food pantry, it's where I get to interact with all the visitors that come through the doors. As a new pastor at the church, I wanted to get to know the people in my community. One day I met a man who wanted to meet the pastor. It caught me off-guard because normally I'm the one making conversation. But this time was different. My new friend shared that he was from Ethiopia and was planting a church for Ethiopian immigrants. The meeting appeared to be a divine appointment. So when my friend asked if he could use The Point's space for a worship service, it was a no-brainer. This man's congregation is relatively new, made up of younger families, and the services are conducted in their native language, Tigrinya. Many of these new Ethiopian friends also come to worship at The Point's service to better learn English and then worship in Tigrinya during their own service.

Overnight, The Point Church's outreach grew by more than fifty individuals and provided a glimpse of what God was doing in the small city of Trotwood. Trotwood is only a microcosm of the immigrants and refugees who are arriving all across the United States. Local churches have an opportunity to be on mission in their own city and nations around the world without having to raise the funds to travel overseas for short-term missions. This is not just about growing local churches; it's about expanding the kingdom of God. Empty buildings and empty seats don't have to remain empty!

Other Examples of Outreach on a Budget

A congregation often thinks that outreach means hosting a large event with food, concerts, and games. What if churches paid attention to the community's interests and needs instead? After assessing the needs of the community, let the congregation know those needs. Your members want to help; they just need to know how, when, and where. One of the most rewarding benefits to outreach is the unity that is often created when the whole church works together to reach the neighborhood. Plus, enlisting the church members' hands-on participation saves on costs. Rather than hiring companies to provide simple services, ask your members for help.

The remainder of this chapter will focus on a few more examples of churches doing incredible ministry on small budgets. The hope is that, as pastors or ministry leaders, readers will recognize in these examples similar opportunities for low-budget outreach in their communities. Again and again, amazing outreach can be accomplished by assessing both the needs and the assets of a given community and a given church, taking advantage of the organizations and events already operating or taking place in a community, and making ourselves and our assets available to whatever God has planned for us in our communities.

Outreach on a budget has been in the DNA of Embrace Church since its beginnings. Friday Night Dinners quickly became a weekly event that attracted people yearning for food and human connection. The only resources needed were food and an open home. Folks from all different backgrounds and lifestyles gathered together each week, and these dinners proved successful.

Another example of Embrace ministering on a budget involved reaching out to the neighboring local elementary school. Arlington is composed of almost 30 percent ESL learners, meaning that a large percentage of the students are unable to communicate fluently or learn effectively in English. These students often live in non–English-speaking homes and typically require modified instruction for their courses. Arlington needed tutors to help these students, and members of Embrace began volunteering as tutors at the elementary school, forging a partnership.

In Detroit, a joint collaboration of the Henry Ford Health Alliance Plan and local pastors have created health kiosks, housed in three community churches and several schools, which serve as "a state-of-the-art, interactive diagnostic and educational tool, designed to assess an individual's physical condition and provide a guide for addressing future health care needs." They are designed to assist people in getting helpful information about preventative health care, including information about diabetes, obesity, heart disease and high blood pressure, HIV and AIDS, as well as a local doctor directory, insurance information, and healthy living information.[4]

In Newport News, Virginia, St. Paul and other area churches offer a "Good Friday Dinner & a Movie" to the community. Every Friday, the church opens its doors for its neighbors to enjoy a meal and a movie in a safe environment. Members from participating churches perform all the work involved, and a local charity donates food for the meal.

Did you know that your community may be facing a diaper shortage? Diapers are important, along with wipes and rash creams, because no government program provides them. Yet without diapers, a parent can't put their child in day care. As a result, parents can miss out on job opportunities and schooling, or their child may be placed in unsafe situations. In an article published by *The Atlantic* called "Diaper Dilemma," the author articulates that the problem is bigger than it seems:

> A year's supply of diapers costs $936. That means a single mother working full time at the minimum wage can expect to spend 6 percent of her annual pay on Pampers alone. Meanwhile, the two biggest programs that assist low-income mothers, SNAP (food stamps) and WIC, don't cover diapers or baby wipes. That might be why, in a study of 877 pregnant and parenting women published in *Pediatrics* in 2013, a team of researchers found that needing diapers and not being able to buy them was a leading cause of mental health problems among new moms.[5]

Embrace Church saw this need and decided to do something about it. A layperson and mother of two had a burden for the single moms in her community. It started for her in the summer of 2014, when she heard a news story about a diaper bank that had been robbed in California. The story shocked her, not just because of the robbery, but also because she had never really thought about the resources available to those who needed help diapering their children.

This mom learned that there are no government programs to supply diapers. However, there are 128 diaper banks registered on the National Diaper Bank Network. This is great news, but it still leaves many gaps around the country where this type of service is not available.

Why is this so important? Wearing diapers too long or reusing them can cause diseases and severe discomfort. There is greater chance of child abuse due to young children crying because of the pain diaper rash can cause. Parents find themselves choosing between food, utilities, and diapers. Also, parents spend a great deal more on diapers because they often only have access to convenience stores where prices are much higher.

Having two young children in diapers herself, the mother felt as though she had to take action. So in the fall of 2014, with the help of her husband, she began collecting diapers from churches and various individuals, and on January 26, 2015, they held the first diaper bank at Embrace Church. The church has since held a diaper bank on the last Monday night of every month. They have had the privilege to assist over 150 families and countless children. The mother who started it all continuously hears from individuals and receives e-mails about the great need for diapers in the Lexington area.

The church has expanded the diaper bank in order to provide a more consistent and dependable supply each month, now giving out forty diapers per child and one package of wipes as available. Today, several thousand diapers have been given away and each month, Embrace serves an average of fifty families. This effort was not carried out in isolation, but rather in partnership with other churches and organizations. Volunteers from the church and other partners are able to spend quality time with children and parents, providing needed encouragement, prayer, and direction to other community resources.

Jim and Kathi Sitzman are a couple in their sixties who exemplify that the best resources of a local church are people. Kathi has never had a brand-new car in her life. Jim has, but the most recent time was 1974. Even though they could afford to purchase new vehicles, they choose instead to fix up harshly weathered cars like Plymouths. Jim and Kathi believe no car is too far gone. In fact, the Sitzmans' hobby was bringing home cars to fix up. At one point, they had about thirty cars on their property! Twenty-one years ago, the couple realized they could help others with their car hobby, so they started the CAR (Christian Auto Redemption) program. CAR's goal is to help elevate people out of poverty by providing a vehicle for transportation in hopes of gainful employment.

Every Thursday and Saturday morning Jim and Kathi bring life to cars that many think will never be road-worthy again. To date, more than six hundred cars have been given away, worth more than two hundred thousand dollars! The requirements to receive a car are fairly straightforward. Participants have two options. They can pay greatly reduced monthly car payments of as little as twenty-five or fifty dollars, which funds CAR ministry costs. Or participants can complete service as payment for the vehicle by serving at New Path or Ginghamsburg Church. A local car dealership has gotten involved, donating one car every quarter because they believe in the ministry of CAR.

The Sitzmans also understand that responsibilities come with car ownership. In order to qualify for CAR, participants need to volunteer and take classes on budgeting and car maintenance. All participants take a Life Skills class. Once clients are back on their feet, New Path encourages an in-kind gift so that others can be served.

The Sitzmans have never been paid a penny for their work. What they get is satisfaction. On the walls of their shop are hundreds of cards and messages from the folks they have helped. It's a reminder why they do what they do. They have no plans to retire anytime soon—in their opinion, there are too many cars that need to be fixed! The Sitzmans didn't need to go through layers of committee approval, have seminary degrees, or obtain the help of paid staff members and clergy to accomplish their God-sized dream. They simply needed to be encouraged to use their gifts to bless others.

There are many people like the Sitzmans who have time, talents, and treasure waiting to be used. Local churches have plumbers, electricians, mechanics, doctors, graphic design artists, and a whole host of talented people who want to use their gifts not only to bless the people in the local church but also as an outreach to their communities.

How many loaves do *you* have? The ingredients of a miracle are right in our midst. The problem is not recognizing it. Members of the clergy and laity alike think they do not have enough, are not smart enough, or are not talented enough. It's amazing what God does with our "not enough" when we offer it to God.

Jesus tells his disciples to bring the leftovers. Why? Twelve disciples and twelve basketfuls. The power of the text is not just what the crowd ate but also what was left over. You can be in the presence of the miracles, or even be used to distribute the miracle, and still not recognize who the miracle giver is. Jesus then sent them into a storm. They carried the evidence of the day's miracle into the storm with them. It was a reminder to the disciples. This was the first mass miracle. Hours later when the storm hit, the leftovers were a reminder to the disciples of God's provision. No matter how much or how little they had, God was faithfully calling them to minister to all people. It's amazing what God can do when you offer God all you have, even as something as little as five loaves and two fish.

NOTES

Introduction

1. "Book of Discipline Section 1: The Churches," The United Methodist Church, accessed November 16, 2015, www.umc.org /what-we-believe/section-1-the-churches.

1. Why So Hungry?

1. Alan Rudnick, "The Case for the 45 Credit Seminary Degree," *Baptist News Global*, July 29, 2014, accessed August 22, 2015, https://baptistnews.com/perspectives/the-case-for-the-45-credit -seminary-degree/.

2. Ibid.

3. David R. Wheeler, "Higher Calling, Lower Wages: The Vanishing of the Middle-Class Clergy," *The Atlantic*, July 22, 2014, accessed October 21, 2015, www.theatlantic.com/busi ness/archive/2014/07/higher-calling-lower-wages-the-collapse -of-the-middle-class-clergy/374786/.

4. Ibid.

5. Andrew Soergel, "1 in 3 Americans Near Financial Disaster," *U.S. News & World Report*, February 23, 2015, accessed October 21, 2015, www.usnews.com/news/blogs/data-mine/2015/02/23 /study-suggests-1-in-3-americans-flirting-with-financial-disaster.

6. "What Are These Programs?" IBR Info, accessed October 21, 2015, http://www.ibrinfo.org/what.vp.html.

7. Martin E. Marty, "Vanishing Clergy," The University of Chicago Divinity School, July 27, 2015, accessed October 22, 2015, https://divinity.uchicago.edu/sightings/vanishing-clergy.

8. Stanley Hauerwas, John Berkman, and Michael G. Cartwright, "Abortion," *The Hauerwas Reader* (Durham, NC: Duke UP, 2001), 609.

9. Shane Claiborne, "Jubilee Party on Wall Street," *Two Cents*, October 21, 2012, accessed July 22, 2015, http://two cents.co/2012/10/21/jubileeparty2012/.

10. Wes McAdams, "Why Churches Should Rethink Their Preacher's Salary," *Radically Christian*, September 9, 2015, accessed October 22, 2015, www.radicallychristian.com/why -churches-should-rethink-their-preachers-salary.

11. RaeAnn Slaybaugh, "Business Training for Pastors Is Gaining Ground," *Church Executive*, December 2, 2013, accessed September 18, 2015, http://churchexecutive.com/archives/busi ness-training-for-pastors-is-gaining-ground.

12. "American Donor Trends," Barna Group, April 12, 2013, accessed October 22, 2015, https://www.barna.org/barna-up date/culture/606-american-donor-trends#.VydklSMrJhE.

13. Joseph Yoo, "When Pastors Don't Give," *Ministry Matters*, January 26, 2015, accessed October 22, 2015, www.ministry matters.com/all/entry/5728/when-pastors-dont-give.

14. LeAnn Snow Flesher, "Low Wages, Student Debt, and 'The Call': Financing Seminary Education," *Sojourners*, July 28, 2014, accessed July 22, 2015, https://sojo.net/articles/low-wages -student-debt-and-call-financing-seminary-education.

15. "How Churches Spend Their Money," Pacific Northwest UMC News Blog, December 2, 2014, accessed June 22, 2015, www.pnwumc.org/news/how-churches-spend-their-money/.

16. Charles Honey, "A Grand Rapids Church Chooses People over Historic Space," *Faith & Leadership*, August 25, 2015,

accessed September 22, 2015, www.faithandleadership.com /grand-rapids-church-chooses-people-over-historic-space.

17. Rosario Picardo, "A Bi-vocational Prognosis," *Ministry Makeover: Recovering a Theology for Bi-vocational Service in the Church* (Eugene, OR: Wipf & Stock, 2015), 84–85.

18. "How Churches Spend Their Money," Pacific Northwest UMC News Blog, December 2, 2014, accessed June 22, 2015, www.pnwumc.org/news/how-churches-spend-their-money/.

19. Lindsey Foster Stringer, "Introducing the Minister of Finance: A Challenge to Pastors," *Ministry Matters*, August 17, 2015, accessed October 22, 2015, www.ministrymatters.com/all /entry/6262/introducing-the-minister-of-finance-a-challenge-to -pastors.

2. Mission Drives Ministry

1. David Synder, "See No Evil," *USCatholic.org*, January 2008, accessed November 16, 2015, www.uscatholic.org/culture /social-justice/2008/06/see-no-evil.

3. Using Your Assets

1. Bruce Peterson, "What Would Wesley Do?" Mount Vernon University, accessed October 12, 2015, www.mvnu.edu /johnaknight/2014papers/petersen-jak-2014.pdf.

2. John Wesley, and Charles Wesley, "Question 74," *The Nature, Design, and General Rules, of the United Societies in London, Bristol, Kingswood, and Newcastle upon Tyne* (Bristol: Printed by Felix Farley, 1743), N. pag.

3. "New Tool Is a Good Place to Start," *Disciples CEF*, August 21, 2013, accessed November 16, 2015, www.disciplescef .org/2013/08/21/new-tool-is-a-good-place-to-start/.

4. Cheryl Truman, "Arlington Studios to bring moderate-priced apartments to North Limestone," *Lexington Herald-Leader*,

November 8, 2014, http://www.kentucky.com/news/local /article44522085.html.

5. Sam Newhouse, "Local Church Offers New Arts Programs to Neighborhood Kids," *The Star*, November 20, 2013, accessed October 12, 2015, www.northeasttimes.com/2013/nov/20/local -church-offers-new-arts-programs-neighbor2/#.VhxXk7zcpSW.

6. Brady Dale, "Why This Church Opened Its Own Coworking Space," *Technical.ly Brooklyn*, November 12, 2014, accessed October 12, 2015, http://technical.ly/brooklyn/2014/11/12/st -lydias-coworking/.

7. Sherri Welch, "Group Links Low-Use Religious Sites with Space-Needy Organizations," *Crain's Detroit Business*, May 17, 2015, accessed October 12, 2015, www.crainsdetroit.com /article/20150517/NEWS/305179971/group-links-low-use-reli gious-sites-with-space-needy-organizations.

8. The Garden Church, accessed October 10, 2015, http:// gardenchurchsp.org/about-us/.

9. "Ten Spaces Every Church Can Share," SPACES by Share-MySpace, November 18, 2013, accessed October 12, 2015, http:// blog.sharemyspace.com/ten-spaces-every-church-can-share/.

4. Partners

1. Tom Eblen, "West Sixth Brewery finds community focus is good for business," *Kentucky.com*, February 1, 2015, http://www .kentucky.com/news/business/article44550894.html.

2. Ibid.

3. "Food Deserts," United States Department of Agriculture Economic Research Service, accessed September 29, 2015, http:// americannutritionassociation.org/newsletter/usda-defines-food -deserts.

4. "USDA ERS—Food Security in the U.S.: Measurement," *USDA ERS—Food Security in the U.S.: Measurement*, United

States Department of Agriculture Economic Research Service, September 29, 2015, www.ers.usda.gov/topics/food-nutrition -assistance/food-security-in-the-us/measurement.aspx.

5. John P. Joseph, "The Two Shall Become One," *Enrichment Journal*, accessed October 12, 2015, http://enrichmentjournal .ag.org/201001/201001_000_Church_Merger.cfm.

6. "When Churches Merge," *Leadership Network*, accessed October 12, 2015, http://leadnet.org/when_churches_merge/.

7. "Equip_Jan2015," *Equip_Jan2015*, West Ohio Conference of The United Methodist Church, accessed November 16, 2015, www.westohioumc.org/sites/default/files/PDF/equip/2015jan /index.html.

8. Joely Johnson Mork, "Coming Together for the Kingdom," *Faith & Leadership*, August 11, 2014, accessed October 12, 2015, www.faithandleadership.com/coming-together-kingdom.

9. John Iwasaki, "2 Very Different Seattle Churches Decide to Unite," June 3, 2007, accessed October 1, 2015, www.seattlepi .com/local/article/2-very-different-Seattle-churches-decide-to -unite-1239472.php.

10. Cindy Gregorson, "St. Croix Valley UMC's Heroic Act Paves Way for Twin Cities Campus of Embrace," Minnesota Annual Conference of The United Methodist Church, August 24, 2015, accessed September 1, 2015, http://www.minnesotaumc .org/newsdetail/st-croix-valley-umc-s-heroic-act-paves-way-for -twin-cities-campus-of-embrace-2575953.

11. "Exciting Faith Community at Fort McKinley Campus," Ginghamsburg Church, accessed September 6, 2015, http://ging hamsburg.org/bring/locations/fort-mckinley-campus.

12. Northwest Children's Outreach, accessed October 12, 2015, www.northwestchildrensoutreach.org/index.php.

13. Kristen Milhollin, "Detroit's Bankruptcy: Churches, Nonprofits, and Entrepreneurs Band Together to Revive Fallen

City," GoodSpeaks, The Good Speaks Project, accessed October 12, 2015, www.goodspeaks.org/event/detroits-bankruptcy -churches-nonprofits-and-entrepreneurs-band-together-to -revive-fallen-city.

14. East Cooper Faith Network: Working Together to Impact Our Community, accessed October 12, 2015, http://ecfaithnet work.org/i-beam/.

15. Stacey Boyd, "Extracurriculars Are Central to Learning," *U.S. News & World Report*, April 28, 2014, accessed October 12, 2015, www.usnews.com/opinion/articles/2014/04/28/music-art -and-language-programs-in-schools-have-long-lasting-benefits.

16. David Whiting, "The Beat Goes On: Churches, Non-profits and Strangers Help Keep the Dream of Music Alive for O.C. Students," *The Orange County Register*, August 10, 2015, accessed October 12, 2015, www.ocregister.com/articles/music -676859-students-santos.html.

17. Dream Center, accessed October 12, 2015, www.dream center.org/about-us/about-us/history/.

18. Jeff Brumley, "Florida Church Builds Partnerships with Schools, Nonprofits—and Laundromats," *Baptist News Global*, February 9, 2015, accessed October 12, 2015, https://baptist news.com/2015/02/09/jacksonville-church-builds-partnerships -with-schools-non-profits-and-laundromats/.

5. Fund-Raising and Grants for Projects

1. "American Donor Trends," Barna Group, April 12, 2013, accessed October 22, 2015, www.barna.org/component /content/article/36-homepage-main-promo/606-barna -update-02-19-2013#.VfwhpxHBzGe.

2. Steven Dilla, "Churches Need a New Giving Model," FaithStreet.com, September 10, 2014, accessed October 12, 2015, www.faithstreet.com/onfaith/2014/09/10/churches-need-a -new-giving-model/34017.

3. Jason Vernon, "10 Things People Want Before They Will Give to Your Church," TonyMorganLive.com, September 24, 2013, accessed October 12, 2015, https://tonymorganlive.com/2013/09/24/10-things-people-want-know-before-they-will-give/.

4. Karen Smith, "Changing Lives One Drop at a Time," *Good News Magazine*, July 8, 2013, accessed October 12, 2015, http://goodnewsmag.org/2013/07/changing-lives-one-drop-at-a-time/>.

5. "The Sudan Project," Ginghamsburg Church, accessed September 8, 2015, http://ginghamsburg.org/serve/ways-to-serve/the-sudan.

6. Daniel Im, "Crowdfunding, Kickstarter, and The Future of Training Church Planters," *The Exchange*, April 9, 2015, accessed October 22, 2015, www.christianitytoday.com/edstetzer/2015/april/crowdfunding-kickstarter-and-future-of-training-church-plan.html.

7. "Neighbors Helping Neighbors," New Path, January 10, 2015, accessed August 12, 2015, http://newpathoutreach.org/neighbors-helping-neighbors-new-path.

8. The Housing Source, a program of CountyCorp in Dayton, Ohio.

6. Outreach on a Budget

1. "Benefits of a Police Ride-Along for Pastors," Personal interview, November 21, 2014.

2. James P. Long, "10 Ways to Make a Big Impact on a Small Budget," OutreachMagazine.com, December 11, 2014, accessed October 12, 2015, www.outreachmagazine.com/resources/small-church-america/4248-big_impact_small_budget.html/1.

3. John L. Easter, "The Indigenous Church: Advancing Our Missions Strategy for the Next 100 Years," *Enrichment*

Journal, accessed September 5, 2015, http://enrichment journal.ag.org/201404/201404_086_Indigenous_Church.cfm. Indigenous Leaders—"Responding to the dilemma created by the dependency system, Henry Venn and Rufus Anderson, two missionary statesmen, initiated the modern concept of the indigenous church. In their view, the ideal goal of Protestant missions was planting the Church on foreign fields through preaching the gospel, cultivating leadership, and developing indigenous churches. They articulated the now-famous three-self formula to describe an indigenous church: self-governing, self-supporting, and self-propagating. The Venn/Anderson model of missions offered a radical departure from the old paradigm."

4. Kristin Milhollin, "Detroit's Bankruptcy: Churches, Nonprofits, and Entrepreneurs Band Together to Revive Fallen City," GoodSpeaks, accessed October 12, 2015, www.goodspeaks.org/event/detroits-bankruptcy-churches-nonprofits-and-entrepreneurs-band-together-to-revive-fallen-city.

5. Olga Khazan, "The Diaper Dilemma," *The Atlantic,* July 21, 2015, accessed October 4, 2015, www.theatlantic.com/health/archive/2015/07/diaper-need/399041/.

CPSIA information can be obtained
at www.ICGtesting.com
Printed in the USA
LVOW01s0729160816

500519LV00005B/5/P